Sharing the Transition to College Workbook

A Collection of Worksheets, Activities and Real-World Scenarios for the College-Bound Student

Copyright © 2022 by Jennifer Sullivan
fastforwardcollegecoaching.com
Published by Tide Pool Books

ISBN: 978-1-7355218-1-7
All rights reserved.
Printed in the United States of America

Limited Photocopy License:
Individual purchasers of this manual have limited rights to photocopy for personal and classroom use only. The worksheet pages may not be reproduced for any other purpose including the following: resale, redistribution, electronic display, books, pamphlets, articles, blogs, file sharing sites, Internet or intranet sites, handouts for lectures, slide shows, webinars, workshops, and therapy groups, whether or not a fee is charged.

Thank you for honoring the authors' substantial time and effort that went into the development of these materials.

The names and incidents used in the examples are fictitious.
Any resemblance to actual persons or events is entirely coincidental.

Sharing the Transition to College Workbook

Jennifer Sullivan
&
Jacquelynn Connell

For more resources to support college-bound students, please visit:
FastForwardCollegeCoaching.com

Welcome!

Dear Educators, Students, Parents & Professionals:

We are excited you found this workbook to support your own, or your students', paths to college. This comprehensive workbook encourages students to improve specific skills and work through situational examples that are necessary for students to have a successful college experience. The reflection questions and activities in this workbook are designed to help identify skills and strengths students are using right now and think about how they can be improved and applied in college. We know that most students don't know what to expect when they go off to college and that's ok, it's the entire point of this workbook! These pages are filled with real-world scenarios that will help prepare students for the exciting journey after high school.

With the average student spending about 15 hours a week in the classroom, a majority of being at college takes place outside of academic buildings. We have intentionally developed activities that cover important skill areas for student life in every aspect of the college experience including practicing difficult conversations with a roommate, managing time and priorities, knowing when and how to ask for help, how to communicate with professional staff and much more!

The worksheets and activities in this workbook were designed specifically for college-bound students. This workbook is intended to make the lives of busy teachers, school counselors, school psychologists, parents, administrators and transition professionals a little easier by providing resources to amplify your incredible work with students.

This workbook provides 89 pages of skill-building activities that will have students feeling more prepared to take on their college experience. Each skill area is introduced and practiced in multiple worksheets. This repetition is intentional to address the unique learning styles of students in your classroom. In addition, many activities require students to explore a college's website to research specific departments and offices. College is a big deal and we feel students should be active and engaged team members as they prepare for their next step - making the lives of students, parents & educators easier. Win-win!

~Jen & Jackie

What's Inside This Workbook

This workbook contains 89 activities and real-world scenarios that will improve students' skills in preparation for college. A few highlights we want to share with you:

Worksheet Design
The workbook pages are designed in black and white so any educator with access to a photocopier can use the worksheets with their students. We know that color ink is expensive! A short description at the top of each page is provided to give context and background to each skill.

Workbook Layout
Worksheets can be completed in any order you choose based on your students' needs and skill development. The workbook is divided into 4 parts (or sections). Part 1 - The first 30 worksheets are based on activities from Jennifer Sullivan's book, Sharing the Transition to College: Words of Advice for Diverse Learners and Their Families. It is not necessary to have read the book in order to understand these first 30 worksheets but the book does offer more detail for students and parents. Part 2 - Workbook exclusive academic and executive functioning skill building worksheets. Part 3 - Workbook exclusive self-advocacy, self-awareness, communication and understanding learning supports skill building worksheets. Part 4 - Workbook exclusive handouts and templates.

Social Emotional Learning
A successful college experience requires students to respond to change, reflect on performance and think creatively about new paths forward, be resilient and persistent in the face of adversity and develop healthy coping strategies when feeling anxiety or stress. Many activities in this workbook include a component of social emotional skill building - designed with social workers and school counselors in mind!

Evidence-Based Activities
The skills in this workbook are based on Jennifer Sullivan's research and experience teaching, advising and coaching undergraduate students across numerous colleges and universities. Jennifer researched evidence-based approaches that lead to students' postsecondary success, identified and embedded these essential components in her own work, and developed this workbook of learning activities that have been successful and effective with students in high school and college.

Student Learning Styles and Preferences
Activities and exercises have been included in a variety of formats. Worksheets include formats that allow for students to write their responses in sentences or short answers, circle their preferences, fill in bubbles or draw pictures including words, symbols or images. This universal approach to learning addresses a wide variety of student learning styles!

Executive Functioning Skill Development
Research indicates that executive functioning skills play an integral role in students' postsecondary success and development of these skills before arriving in higher education is ideal. Real-world scenarios are incorporated throughout the workbook placing a strong emphasis on developing students' time management, organization, planning, prioritization, and task initiation skills.

Table of Contents

Exercises From the Book, "Sharing the Transition to College"

1. Check the College's Social Media Accounts
2. Show Up for Class a Few Minutes Early
3. Communicate with Your Roommate
4. Be Prepared for Less Privacy
5. Know the Phone Number of the Campus Safety Office
6. The Power of Multiples - Bring 1, 2, or 3
7. Be Persistent
8. Explore Assistive Technology, Especially if You've Never Tried it Before
9. Ask for Help
10. Know the Names and Contact Info of Your Resident Assistants (RAs)
11. Find the Best Place for You to do Homework
12. Pick One Day Every Week to Do Your Laundry (Clothes & Bedding!)
13. Respect Your Roommate's Space
14. Even if You Put in a Lot of Effort, College Might Still Be Hard
15. Find Out Where the Health & Counseling Centers are Located
16. Keep a Consistent Sleep Schedule
17. Keep Important Personal Items in a Drawer Out of Sight
18. Write Down Usernames and Passwords for Your College Accounts
19. Personal Hygiene - Keep it Private
20. Know When to Contact Your RA, Campus Safety, or Call 911
21. Visit Each Professor at Least Once During the Semester in Their Office
22. Put Yourself in Social Situations – Even if it's Uncomfortable
23. Know Your Learning Style
24. Speaking Up for Yourself is Important
25. Remember to Keep Your Devices Charged
26. Understand How Your Disability Affects You
27. If You Need Accommodations, Ask for Them
28. Visit the Campus Accessibility Office - It's a Great Resource!
29. Be Independent, But Don't be Too Proud to Ask for Help
30. Don't Guess How You're Doing in your Classes – Find Out!

Academic & Executive Functioning Skill Building

31. Assignment Planning
32. Task Initiation & Doing Things We Don't Want To
33. Scheduling & Morning Routine
34. Textbook Options & Preferences
35. Express Yourself: Procrastination
36. College Writing Exercise
37. High School vs. College
38. Real-World Time Management & Organization Scenarios
39. Time to Get Organized
40. Your Phone as a Support Resource

Table of Contents Continued

Academic & Executive Functioning Skill Building Continued

41	Time Waster Assessment
42	Time Management, Organization & Scheduling
43	Breaking Down Large Projects - Part One
44	Breaking Down Large Projects - Part Two
45	Breaking Down Large Projects - Part Three
46	Self-Advocacy & Time Management Scenarios
47	Procrastination at College
48	Prioritizing College Assignments - Part One
49	Prioritizing College Assignments - Part Two

Self-Awareness, Self-Advocacy, Connecting to Campus Resources & Communication Skill Building

50	Campus Health & Wellness
51	Roommate Communication
52	Questions to Ask Campus Accessibility Offices
53	Self-Reflection
54	Self-Awareness
55	Healthy Transitions - Part One
56	Healthy Transitions - Part Two
57	Know Your Campus Mental Health Resources
58	Self-Disclosure at College
59	Understanding Your 504/IEP & Preparing for College
60	Self-Advocacy & Communicating with Professors
61	Conversations With Your Roommate - Part One
62	Conversations With Your Roommate - Part Two
63	Express Yourself: Self Check-in
64	Talking About a Disability
65	Staying Physically Healthy at College
66	Connecting to Campus Outside of the Classroom
67	Living on Your Own - The Good, the Bad & the Dirty
68	Self-Awareness & Bringing Your Strengths to College
69	Basics in Money Management
70	Don't Forget to Meet the Deadlines
71	What is Your Communication Style?
72	Stress is Normal. Let's Talk About it!
73	Discipline vs. Distractions
74	Problem Solving in College - Part One
75	Problem Solving in College - Part Two
76	Express Yourself: Forward Thinking
77	College Website Scavenger Hunt
78	Dealing With Noise in Your Residence Hall

Workbook Exclusive Handouts

79	Daily Planner
80	Weekly Planner
81	Executive Functioning
82	College Disability Support Services
83	Sample Accommodations Letter
84	Examples of Accommodations
85	Make Your Goals SMART
86	Not-To-Do-List
87	Semester Class Schedule
88	College Application Tracker
89	Important Contacts

Want to address a specific skill?

The activities in this workbook focus on essential skill areas for college-bound students to assess, build and practice the competencies necessary to be successful in college. The Index on the pages following the table of contents clearly and conveniently lay out the skills addressed in each activity.

Workbook Exercise Skill Index

Student Tip Workbook Exercise	Time Management, Organization & Goals	Self-Advocacy	Communication & Being Social	Campus Resources	Academic Life	Mental & Physical Health	Self-Awareness	Disability Related	Residence Life
1 College's Social Media				X					
2 Show Up Early	X				X				
3 Communicate with Roommate			X			X			X
4 Less Privacy			X			X			X
5 Campus Safety Phone Number				X					X
6 Power of Multiples	X								X
7 Be Persistent					X	X			
8 Explore Assistive Technology						X	X		
9 Ask for Help		X	X						
10 Know the Name of Your RA		X	X						X
11 Find Where to do Homework					X	X			
12 Pick 1x Per Week For Laundry									X
13 Respect Your Roommate's Space		X	X			X			X
14 College Might Still Be Hard					X				
15 Research Health & Counseling Centers			X		X				X
16 Keep Consistent Sleep Schedule	X								X
17 Keep Important Items Out of Sight									X
18 Write Down Login/Password	X				X				

Workbook Exercise Skill Index

Student Tip Workbook Exercise	Time Management, Organization & Goals	Self-Advocacy	Communication & Being Social	Campus Resources	Academic Life	Mental & Physical Health	Self-Awareness	Disability Related	Residence Life
19 Personal Hygiene						X		X	
20 Contacting RA, Campus Safety, 911				X					X
21 Visit Professors 1x/Semester		X	X	X	X				
22 Put Yourself in Social Situations			X	X					
23 Know Your Learning Style					X		X		
24 Speak Up for Yourself		X	X				X	X	
25 Keep Devices Charged	X				X			X	
26 How Your Disability Affects You		X			X		X	X	X
27 Accommodations, Ask for Them		X			X		X		
28 Accessibility Office is a Great Resource				X	X		X		
29 Be Independent, But Ask for Help		X					X		
30 Don't Guess How You're Doing, Ask!		X			X	X			
31 Assignment Planning	X				X				
32 Doing What We Don't Want to Do	X				X	X			
33 Scheduling & Morning Routine	X				X			X	
34 Textbook Options & Preferences					X		X		
35 Express Yourself: Procrastination	X				X		X		
36 College Writing Exercise					X		X		

Workbook Exercise Skill Index

Exclusive Workbook Exercise	Time Management, Organization & Goals	Self-Advocacy	Communication & Being Social	Campus Resources	Academic Life	Mental & Physical Health	Self-Awareness	Disability Related	Residence Life
37 High School vs. College				X			X		
38 Real Time Mgmt & Organization	X				X				
39 It's Time to Get Organized	X				X				
40 Your Phone as a Support Resource	X				X	X		X	
41 Time Waster Assessment	X				X		X		X
42 Time Mgmt., Org. & Scheduling	X				X				
43 Breaking Down Projects - Part 1	X				X				
44 Breaking Down Projects - Part 2	X				X				
45 Breaking Down Projects - Part 3	X				X				
46 Self-Advocacy & Time Mgmt.	X	X			X				
47 Procrastination at College	X				X				
48 Prioritizing Assignments-Part 1	X				X				
49 Prioritizing Assignments-Part 2	X				X				
50 Campus Health & Wellness				X		X			
51 Roommate Communication		X	X						X
52 Questions to Ask a Disability Office		X		X	X			X	
53 Self-Reflection							X		
54 Self-Awareness					X		X		

Workbook Exercise Skill Index

Exclusive Workbook Exercise	Time Management, Organization & Goals	Self-Advocacy	Communication & Being Social	Campus Resources	Academic Life	Mental & Physical Health	Self-Awareness	Disability Related	Residence Life
55 Healthy Transitions - Part 1		X		X		X	X	X	
56 Healthy Transitions - Part 2		X		X		X	X	X	
57 Campus Mental Health Resources				X		X		X	
58 Self-Disclosure at College		X	X					X	
59 Understanding Your 504/IEP		X				X	X	X	
60 Self-Advocacy with Professors		X	X			X		X	
61 Converse with Roommate - Part 1		X	X						X
62 Converse with Roommate - Part 2		X	X						X
63 Express Yourself: Self-Check in							X		
64 Talking About a Disability		X					X	X	
65 Staying Physically Healthy at College						X			
66 Connecting Out of the Classroom				X					
67 Living on Your Own Good, Bad & Dirty									X
68 Bringing Strengths to College					X		X		
69 Basics in Money Management							X		X
70 Don't Forget to Meet Deadlines	X				X				X
71 What is Your Comm. Style?			X				X		
72 Stress is Normal Let's Talk About it					X	X	X		X

Workbook Exercise Skill Index

Exclusive Workbook Exercise	Time Management, Organization & Goals	Self-Advocacy	Communication & Being Social	Campus Resources	Academic Life	Mental & Physical Health	Self-Awareness	Disability Related	Residence Life
73 Discipline vs. Distractions	X				X		X		X
74 Problem Solving in College-Part 1	X		X		X				X
75 Problem Solving in College-Part 2	X		X						X
76 Express Yourself: Forward Thinking							X		
77 College Website Scavenger Hunt				X					
78 Noise in the Residence Hall		X	X				X		X
79 Daily Planner	X				X				
80 Weekly Planner	X				X				
81 Executive Functioning	X				X			X	
82 Disability Support Services	X	X		X	X			X	
83 Accommodation Letter		X		X	X			X	
84 Examples of Accommodations				X	X			X	X
85 SMART Goals	X				X	X			
86 Not-To-Do List	X					X	X		
87 Class Schedule Template	X				X				
88 College Application Tracker	X			X					
89 Important Contacts	X			X	X				X

Exercises From the Book, 'Sharing the Transition to College'

1 EXERCISE

Student Tip: Check the college's social media accounts

From the Book

Activities outside of the classroom create a complete college experience. Colleges want to keep you connected to the activities and events they host, so campus departments utilize many forms of social media to advertise when and where events are happening. Before you arrive on campus, find out how your college promotes involvement opportunities and follow them on social media.

1. Go to your college's website.
2. Find the Student Life or Campus Life section of the website.
3. Search for the ways the college advertises and promotes student activities and events. Do they have an events calendar? Do they use Twitter or other social media channels?

What did you find out? In the spaces below, list the ways your college advertises & promotes campus activities & student events:

2 EXERCISE

Student Tip: Show up for class a few minutes early
(Early is on time, on time is late)

From the Book

The start time of your class is exactly that – the time your class starts. Not a minute later. Arriving to class a few minutes early shows your professor that you think the class is important. Arriving a few minutes late implies that you don't care about the class. Even if you believe the class is important and have good intentions, but often arrive late, a professor who does not know you will only judge you based on your actions, so don't be late!

Alex has an Introduction to College Writing class that starts at 10:00 a.m. on Mondays and Thursdays. Alex likes to shower and eat breakfast in the morning before class. It takes him 20 minutes to walk from his residence hall to the cafeteria on campus. Then it takes Alex 20 minutes to walk from the cafeteria to the academic building on campus where his class is held. Use Alex's schedule below to visualize and answer the questions.

Alex's Schedule

	Monday	Tuesday	Wednesday
8:00			
9:00		Math 105 9-10:30	Meet with Advisor 9:30
10:00	College Writing 10-11:30		
11:00			
12:00			Campus Cookout Noon
1:00		Psychology 1:30-3	
2:00	Humanities 2-3		Humanities 2-3
3:00			
4:00		Communication 4-7	
5:00			Club Meeting 5-???

What time should Alex wake up on Mondays & Thursdays to shower?
_____

What time should Alex leave his residence hall to walk to the cafeteria for breakfast?
_____

What time should Alex leave the cafeteria to be sure he arrives at his Writing class on time?
_____

Alex has very few classes on Wednesdays. What are some other ways he can use that time?
_____
_____
_____

3 EXERCISE

Student Tip: Communicate with your roommate
(Yes, this means you need to talk to them)

From the Book

You don't need to become best friends with your roommate, but you should build a relationship with them. Be prepared for some minor conflicts because when two people share space there will likely be disagreements. Have a conversation at the beginning of the semester to establish guidelines and rules for your room that you both agree upon. If your residence hall provides a roommate agreement form take it seriously when you fill it out and don't assume you will figure things out if issues come up... because they will come up. Effective communication is key to a civil roommate relationship.

Real Life Scenario

Brandon and his roommate, Jay, get along pretty well. They keep their belongings on different sides of the dorm room, but share one mini-refrigerator. Brandon has noticed that his energy drinks are disappearing from the fridge. He assumes that Jay is drinking them and gets angry with Jay, but doesn't say anything, so Brandon eats Jay's chips to, "pay him back". Jay notices that his chips are gone and gets angry with Brandon, but he doesn't say anything. When his friends come over to hang out, Jay tells them to eat Brandon's food because Brandon has been eating his chips.

What are two problems that you see in this scenario?

1. _____
2. _____

Why do you think Brandon and Jay are not talking to each other about why they are upset?

What could happen if the roommates continue to avoid talking about this situation?

How do you think a Resident Assistant (RA) could help them solve this conflict?

EXERCISE 4
Student Tip: Be prepared for less privacy

From the Book

Sharing a room with another student means that two living spaces will coexist in a space typically not much bigger than 10x15 feet. All of the things that you do in your living space will be done with another person nearby, which if you had your own room growing up, will be a new experience. For example, you will sleep a few feet apart, change clothes in the same room as your roommate, and your phone conversations will be overheard by your roommate. You and your roommate should talk about privacy, and what it takes for each of you to feel comfortable.

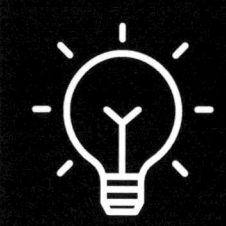

Think About It

What are your privacy expectations? What rules does your family have about privacy in your house? How might your routines change when you get to college? Use the space below to depict your privacy needs when thinking about living with a roommate and sharing communal bathroom spaces.

{ }

If you are planning to share a room with a roommate in college, how could you start a conversation with that person about privacy?

_____
_____
_____

5 EXERCISE

Student Tip: Know the phone number of the Campus Safety office

From the Book

When you are at college, it's very important to know who to call in case of an emergency. Every college and university has security officers who patrol the campus to make sure students and staff are safe. These officers are sometimes called Campus Safety officers or Campus Police.

1. Go to your college's website.
2. Find the Security, Campus Life or Campus Safety section.
3. Search for the initiatives the college has in place to prioritize safety of students and the campus community.
4. Put the Campus Safety phone number in your phone now!

What did you find out? In the spaces below, list how your college promotes safety, the ways students can connect with Campus Safety, and how you can report concerns:

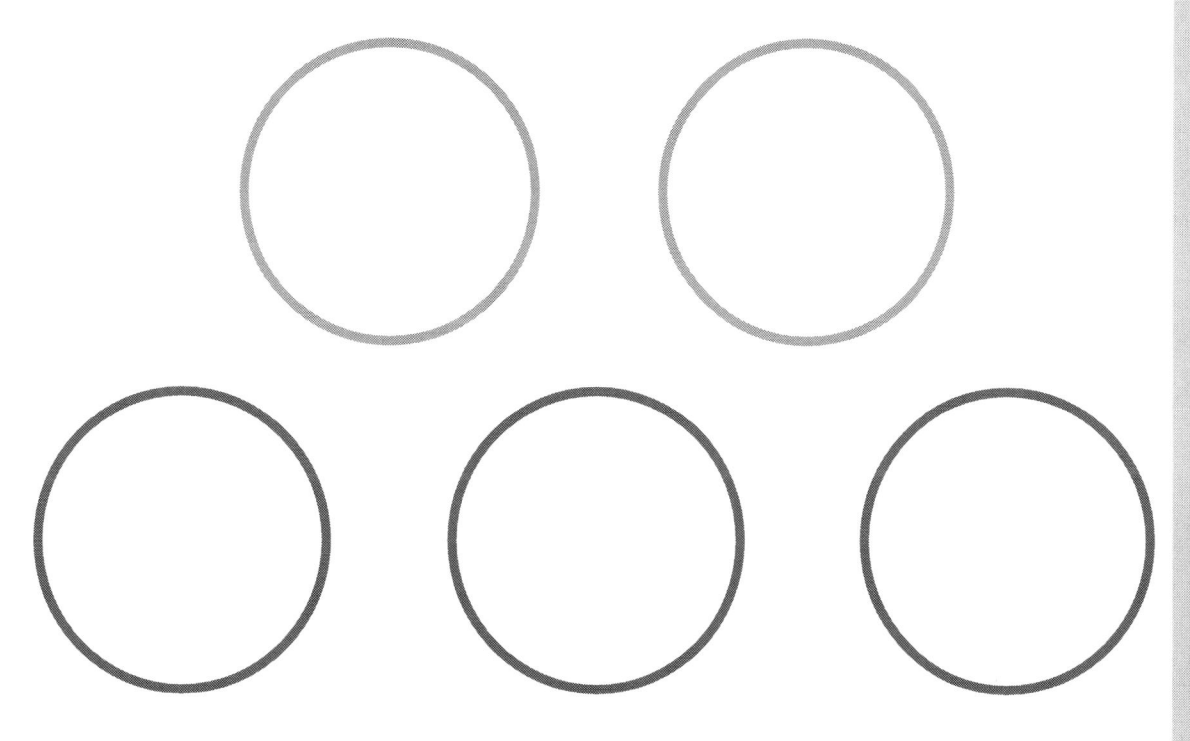

6 EXERCISE

Student Tip: The power of multiples - Bring 1, 2, or 3

From the Book

Phone and computer chargers are extremely important because they power your devices. Remembering to charge your devices is YOUR responsibility. You should not expect there to be charging outlets available in classrooms so you will have to plan ahead to make sure your devices are ready to use. Because charging cords are so important, you should bring more than one with you to college. Students with executive functioning challenges (i.e. organization and memory challenges) may want to place two charging cords in their dorm room in highly visible locations. If the cords are placed in highly visible locations you will be more likely to see them and use them.

Real Life Scenario

Jonathan prefers to type his notes rather than use a notebook and pen. He brings his laptop to every class but, unfortunately, it's often not charged because he forgets to plug it in. He has one charging cord that is under his desk in his dorm room. When Jonathan is in class and his laptop isn't charged, he gets frustrated because he can't take notes.

✏️ What suggestions can you think of that might help Jonathan remember to charge his laptop so he is ready to take notes in class?

_____
_____
_____

✏️ Student stress is real, and it can be more challenging to remember things when we feel stressed out. What strategies do you use when you feel overwhelmed to remember things you need to do and keep track of your belongings?

_____
_____
_____
_____

7 EXERCISE
Student Tip: Be persistent

From the Book

You may experience setbacks and challenging times during your first year at college. Students who expect college to be easy will be in for a surprise! If you know there will be challenging times ahead, then you can prepare yourself, and build your personal toolbox. A personal toolbox can be full of tips, tools, and coping strategies that will help you when college gets difficult. Persistence is one tool that absolutely needs to be in your personal toolbox.

Think About It

What does, "being persistent" mean to you? Are there areas of your life/school where you have demonstrated persistence? Is this an area in which you feel confident, or do you feel your persistence skills could use a little work?

Write two situations when you have demonstrated persistence

1. _____
2. _____

Think about your friends, family & classmates. Identify one person you know who has shown persistence and write their name in the thought bubble.

Now describe a situation where this person has shown persistence.
_____
_____
_____

What actions showed they were persistent?
_____
_____
_____

EXERCISE 8

Student Tip: Explore assistive technology, especially if you've never tried it before

From the Book

Assistive technology (AT) is any item, piece of equipment, or software program that is used to increase, maintain, or improve the capabilities of an individual with a disability. In college, AT is referred to as technology that helps a student access their academic course content and assignments. AT can be no-tech, low-tech, or high-tech.

1. Go to your college's website.
2. Find the Accessibility Office, Student Success Center, or Tutoring Center on the website.
3. Search for academic tools, apps, or technologies that are suggested to students.

What did you find out? In the spaces below, list the academic tools, apps, or technologies the college recommends for student success on their website:

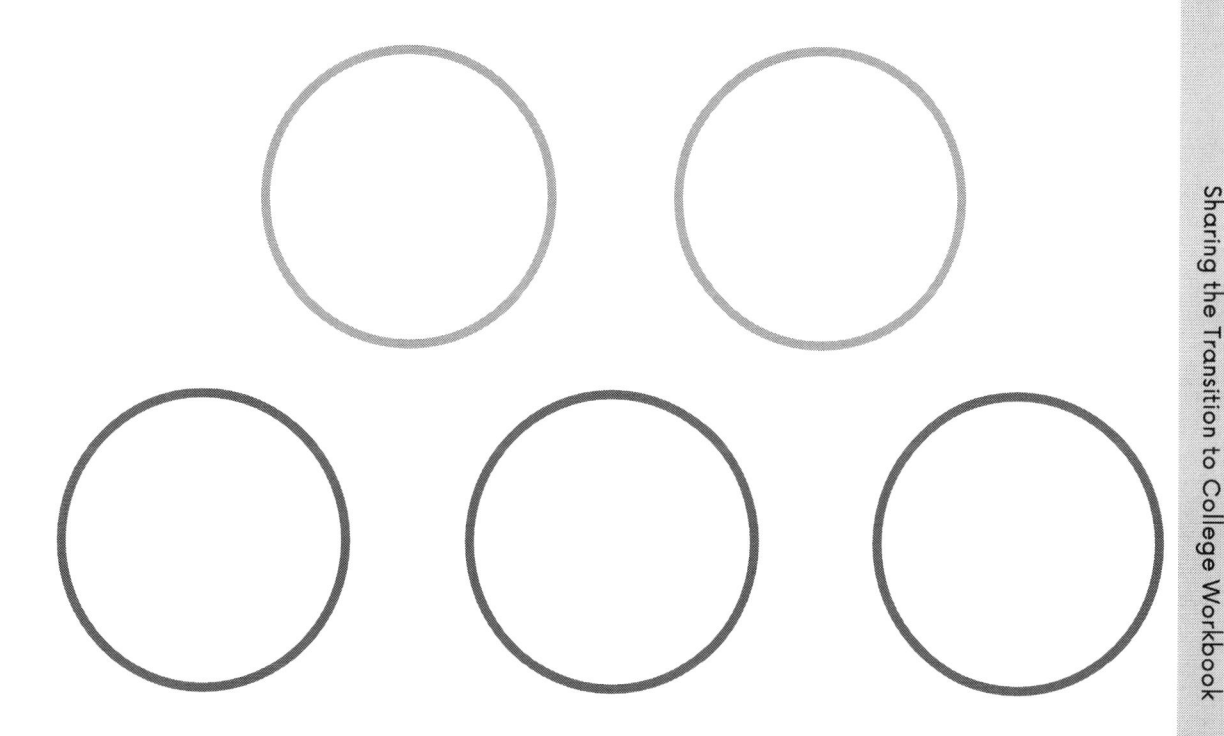

9 EXERCISE
Student Tip: Ask for help

From the Book

Asking for help may sound like a simple thing to do, but some students find it easier said than done. Asking for help requires you to do two things: 1) acknowledge that you need help, and 2) have the courage to ask for it. In college, there are many resources to help you be successful, but YOU have to realize when you need help, and YOU need to ask for it.

Think About It

Research has shown that college students who ask for help when they struggle are more successful than students who don't ask for help. Why do you think students might not ask for help?

Write two situations when you have been reluctant to ask for help

1. _____
2. _____

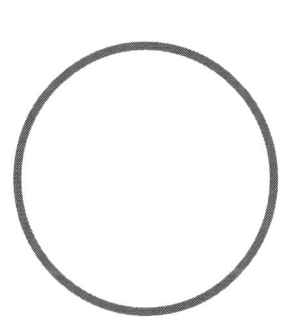

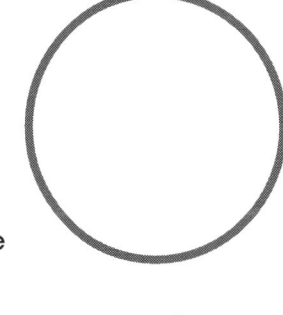

List 3 reasons why students might be reluctant to ask for help

Write 3 positive outcomes that could happen if students ask for help in college

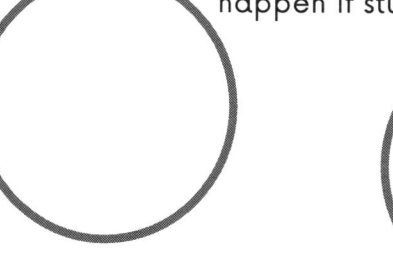

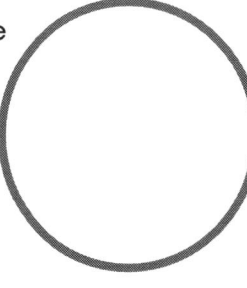

10 EXERCISE

Student Tip: Know the names and contact info of your Resident Assistants (RAs)

From the Book

Resident Assistants (RAs) are student leaders who have responsibilities and leadership roles in the residence halls. They will have a dorm room on your floor or in your residence hall, and are your go-to person if you have questions or needs. RAs are highly trained to build community in your building, assist with roommate issues and connect you to campus resources. RAs should be your first stop and can help with just about everything.

1. Go to your college's website.
2. Search for the Residence Life or Living on Campus section of the website.
3. Research the different types of housing options and residence life support that are present on and off campus.

What did you find out? In the spaces below, list the types of people that work in the Residence Life office and in the residence halls who are there to support students.

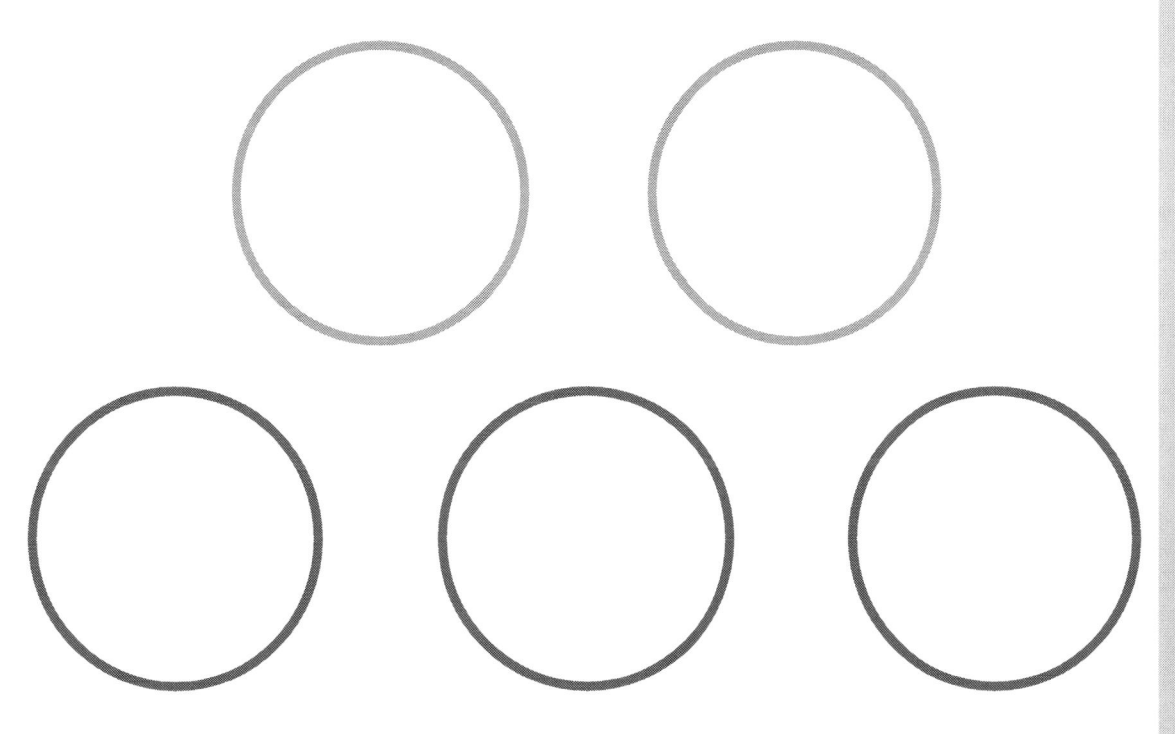

11 EXERCISE
Student Tip: Find the best place to do homework

From the Book

College campuses have many different types of spaces for students to work, hang out, and socialize. Spend some time thinking about your current study and homework habits, and then think about the ideal college environment for you to study and learn. Try a few different spots on campus to find one that makes you feel the most comfortable and productive.

Think About It
When you go to college you will want to find a place to do homework that allows you to be comfortable AND successful. Think about how you do your homework right now as you answer the questions below.

Where do you sit -
At a desk? On your bed?
At a table?
_____
_____

What sounds are nearby -
Do you need complete silence?
Some noise? White noise/music?
_____
_____

Do you like a fan or use a blanket? Do you like being warm or cold to be productive?
_____
_____

What do you see – Do you face a wall, a window, etc.?
_____
_____

Based on your answers, list two places on campus that could be ideal for you to do assignments

1. _____
   _____
   _____

2. _____
   _____
   _____

EXERCISE 12

Student Tip: Pick one day every week to do your laundry (Clothes & Bedding!)

Spraying Febreze™ does not count as "doing laundry"

From the Book

A less talked about (but very important) part of college is personal cleanliness. The way you look and smell can impact your ability to make friends, and develop personal and professional relationships. Shower daily. Choose one day each week, the same day, to do your laundry. Remember, your clothes, towels, bed sheets, AND pillow cases need to be clean if you are to be clean.

Real Life Scenario

Alycia is a student-athlete who plays basketball and has practices or games every night that start around 6:00 p.m. and last until 9:00 p.m. She has classes on Monday, Wednesday and Friday that begin at 10:30 a.m. and last until 5:00 p.m. then she eats dinner before practice. Her classes on Tuesday and Thursday start at 1:10 p.m. and last until 5:45p.m. On the weekends Alycia does not have basketball practice but she likes to sleep in and then go to lunch at 12:00 noon. Alycia follows her team rules about not partying at night, so she usually stays in her dorm room with friends and hangs out on the weekends.

Alycia is having trouble finding a time to do her laundry each week because she is busy with basketball practice and classes.

Thinking about Alycia's schedule, use the clocks below to determine and plot out a time she could start her laundry depending on the day and her other commitments.

Monday/Wed./Friday   Tuesday/Thursday    Saturday/Sunday

If you were Alycia, when would YOU choose to do your laundry?

_____

_____

13 EXERCISE

Student Tip: Respect your roommate's space by keeping your belongings on your side of the room

From the Book

It's important to respect your roommate's space, and accept that half of the room is theirs. Keep your belongings on your side of the room. If you and your roommate have a conversation and agree to share space or belongings, that's great, but don't assume. If you respect your roommate's space, they are more likely to respect yours. If issues arise, your Resident Assistant (RA) can help.

Real Life Scenario

Natalia is a college freshman who lives on campus with her roommate, Madison. On the weekends, Madison goes home so Natalia has the room to herself. Natalia invites a few friends over on the weekends to hang out and listen to music in her dorm room. They usually order pizza and have snacks. One Sunday night, Madison returns to campus and when she enters the dorm room she notices there are food crumbs and chip bag wrappers on her bed. Madison gets upset and asks Natalia why there are crumbs and food wrappers on her bed. Natalia said that she had a few friends over this weekend and it was no big deal.

Why do you think Madison is upset?

_____
_____
_____

What are some topics that Natalia and Madison should talk about in regard to sharing space?

_____
_____
_____
_____

14 EXERCISE

Student Tip: Even if you put in a lot of effort, college might still be hard

From the Book

This tip can be one of the hardest concepts for students to understand. You may have received good grades in high school based, in part, on your effort. In college, things might be different. Professors don't care how long you worked on an assignment. They only care about the finished product. This is a big difference between high school and college. This is one of the reasons that even if you are putting in solid effort, college can still be hard.

Think About It

Difficult situations from high school or other activities were good practice for challenging situations you may have in college (and in life). Remember, don't give up when you face difficult situations. Keep going!

Think about difficult situations you have dealt with in high school. Write down two situations that were hard for you (in school or outside of school) and how you dealt with those tough situations.

Situation One: _____
_____
_____
_____

Situation Two: _____
_____
_____
_____

15 EXERCISE

Student Tip: Find out where the health & counseling centers are located – even if you don't need them now

From the Book

Most colleges and universities have a health/medical center and also counseling services. Even if you don't need to talk with a therapist right now or haven't talked with one in the past, a situation may arise sometime in your college career when you may want to talk with a counselor. Another reason to know the location of your campus counseling center is to be a support for a friend or roommate who may need counseling services.

1. Go to your college's website.
2. Find the Student Life or Campus Life section.
3. Search for the various Health & Wellness services that are offered on campus, both physical and mental health resources. (Examples: Walk-in clinic, peer support groups, 24-hr helplines)

What did you find out? In the spaces below, list the physical and mental health support services listed on the website:

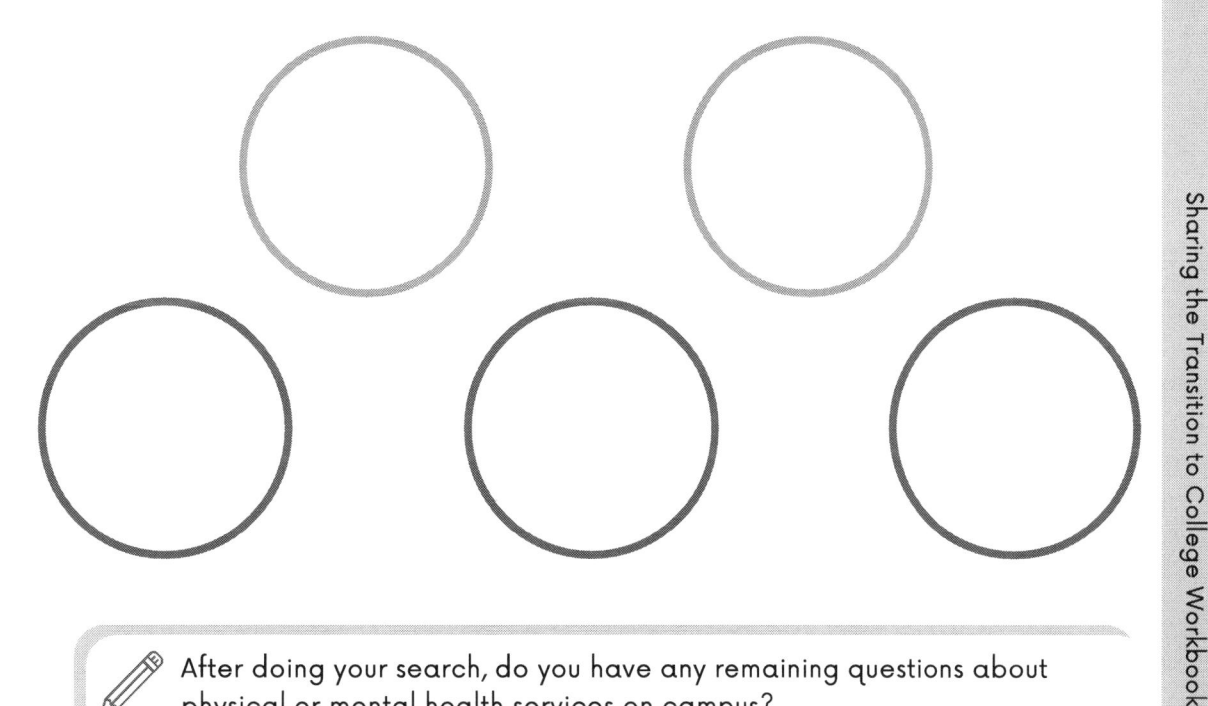

After doing your search, do you have any remaining questions about physical or mental health services on campus?

_____
_____

16 EXERCISE

Student Tip: Keep a consistent sleep schedule

From the Book

A consistent sleep schedule can greatly enhance your college experience by keeping your mind and body functioning in a healthy way. Sleep really does affect your ability to do your best work! Getting enough sleep provides you with the best chance for success. Studies show that losing one night of sleep, perhaps by pulling an all-nighter, can adversely affect your physical and mental health for seven days afterward.

Think About It

Think about your current sleep schedule. How many hours do you usually sleep on weeknights? On the weekends? Do you feel good about that amount or should it change? Think about how much sleep it takes for you to truly feel rested and able to be alert and productive.

Consider your needs when it comes to a sleeping environment that allows you to fall asleep and stay asleep through the night. Fill in the circles below to note your preferences.

Brightness	Volume	Temperature	Other Preferences
○ Lights On	○ No Noise	○ Cooler	○ _____
○ Lights Off	○ Some Noise	○ Warmer	○ _____
○ Other: _____	○ Other: _____	○ Other: _____	○ _____

What is one challenge that you have now to getting enough sleep? (Examples: staying up late watching videos, playing video games, texting, etc.) Identify one way that you will try to overcome this barrier in college.

_____

_____

_____

17 EXERCISE
Student Tip: Keep Important personal items in a drawer out of sight

From the Book

Having a roommate in college means that students you don't know may enter your personal space. It's important to have a secure place in your room to keep your important personal belongings (such as medications, money, etc.). We hope that everyone you meet in college will be honest and trustworthy, but that might not be the case. Colleges recommend that students buy a lock box that requires a key or code to open for their dorm room.

Think About It

When you go to college you will be fully responsible for all of your belongings. Think about what items you consider important (Ex. wallet, phone, jewelry, money, documents, etc.) and about how you keep them safe now (Ex: leave with parent, special drawer/cabinet, backpack, etc.). How might that change?

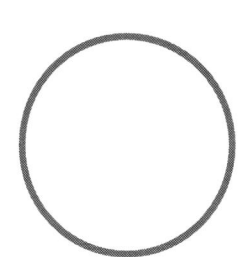

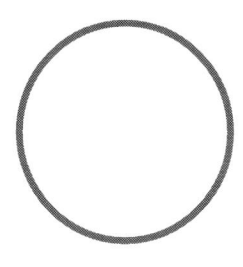

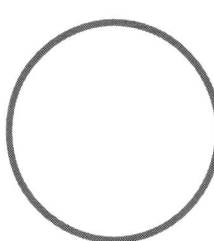

Write some important belongings that you have at home in the circles above

Write where you keep important belongings at home in the circles below

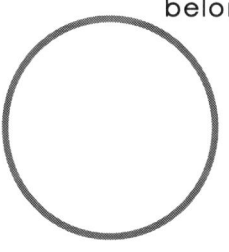

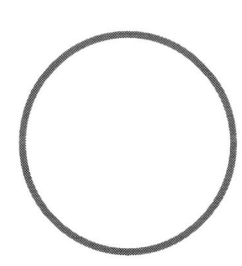

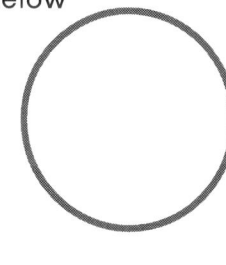

Brainstorm two places that you could put these important belongings when you go to college

1. _____
2. _____

18 EXERCISE

Student Tip: Write down usernames and passwords for your college accounts

From the Book

Each college and university is different, but all schools will assign new college students an email address and most use learning management programs. You will be required to create multiple new accounts, which means new usernames and passwords. Remembering all of your usernames and password can be tough. It's a good idea to find a password storage app or organizational system that you like and works for you BEFORE you arrive on campus.

Think About It

What is the method that you use right now to remember your usernames/passwords? Do you write them in a book, use an app, save them in your email/smartphone? If you have trouble remembering this information that is okay too, but developing a plan before you get to campus will save lockout headaches.

What are the different apps and accounts that you have right now that you need to remember usernames & passwords?
List the programs you login to on the screen below:

You will be required to use your campus email and other new accounts that are given to you by your college. What are some methods that you could use to store or remember your usernames and passwords?

_____
_____

19 EXERCISE

Student Tip: Personal hygiene - Keep it private

From the Book

Getting privacy while living on campus can be tricky. Sharing a room requires that roommates understand and respect each other's personal boundaries. Talk to your roommate at the beginning of the semester about privacy, personal boundaries, and overnight guests even if the conversation is uncomfortable or awkward.

Think About It

Think about personal hygiene routines that you have now and where you do those routines. Where do you shave, change clothes, brush your teeth, comb your hair, take medication, etc.? Maybe you have a medical condition that requires you to do other medical tasks (such as changing a bandage, using a medical device, etc.). If you currently do these personal hygiene tasks in private, you should consider where you will do them in college if you live with a roommate and share a common bathroom with other students in your residence hall.

Use the circles below to list any thoughts or questions on the topic of privacy in your residence hall:

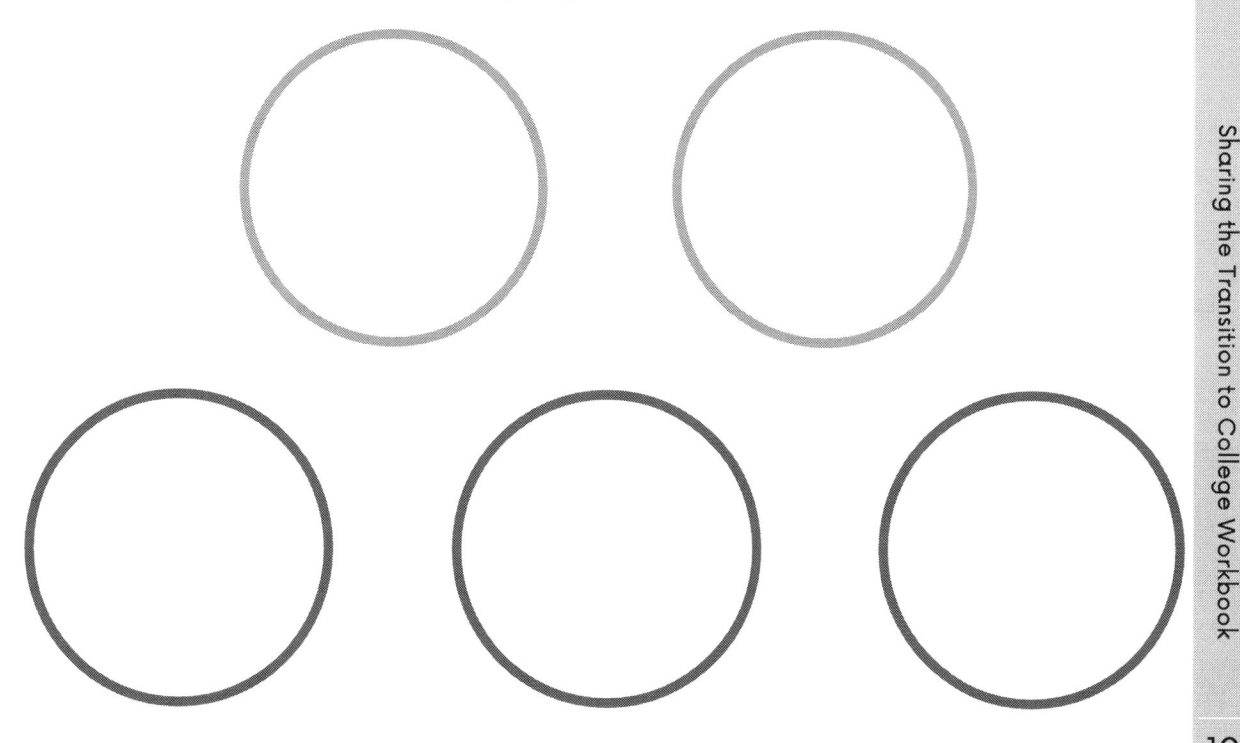

EXERCISE 20

Student Tip: Know when to contact your RA, Campus Safety, or call 911

From the Book

No one wants to imagine that emergencies will happen at college, but occasionally a situation will occur when you need to get help. When you arrive on campus be sure to know the location or building of the Campus Safety office, Residence Life office, Student Union, etc. It's important to know **WHEN** to ask for help and **WHO** to contact for different levels of help. We recommend you put important campus numbers in your phone before you get to campus.

Real Life Scenario

You may have experience resolving conflicts in your high school or at home, but it may take some time to adjust to the support systems at your college, and knowing when and who to ask for help if you need it. Read the scenarios below and identify if the situation would require you to contact your dorm Resident Assistant, Campus Safety or call 911.

Situational Scenarios — Who should you contact?

#	Scenario	Resident Assistant	Campus Safety	911
1	You are attending an Anime Student Club meeting on campus and the meeting ended at 11pm. You feel nervous walking back to your dorm in the dark.	○	○	○
2	You can't get to sleep at night because the room next door is playing loud music. You have asked them to turn the music down, and they said that it is the weekend and they are allowed to have fun.	○	○	○
3	You are hanging out in your friend's dorm room when he starts to have a seizure. You aren't sure what to do because your friend has never had a seizure before.	○	○	○
4	You park your car in a student parking lot and walk to class. When you return to your car it looks like another car hit your car and your taillight is broken and bumper is scratched.	○	○	○

Answers: 1.) Campus Safety, 2.) Resident Assistant, 3.) 911, 4.) Campus Safety

21 EXERCISE
Student Tip: Visit each professor at least once during the semester in their office

From the Book

In college, you WANT professors to know you by name (not just by your ID number), know your learning style, and know how they can help you be successful. Unlike high school, YOU need to make the first move in college. YOU need to schedule appointments with your professors; they will not initiate scheduling appointments with you. So go ahead and schedule a meeting with your professors at least once per semester, even if you don't need any help.

Think About It

Think about your current and previous teachers. You probably liked the teaching style of some teachers more than others. For example, some teachers like to tell stories while others follow an agenda or lesson plan the same way every class. Think about some of your favorite high school teachers. Why did you like them? What was their teaching style?

Use the prompts below to write your thoughts about **WHY** you liked three of your favorite teachers

Teacher #1
Things you liked about them:
___
___
___
___

What was their teaching style?
___
___
___

Teacher #2
Things you liked about them:
___
___
___
___

What was their teaching style?
___
___
___

Teacher #3
Things you liked about them:
___
___
___
___

What was their teaching style?
___
___
___

EXERCISE 22

Student Tip: Put yourself in social situations – even if it's uncomfortable

From the Book

College classes and coursework are important, but college is also about making new friends and exploring social events and activities. Your college friends can provide much needed study breaks and can also be your support system while you are away from home. For students with social anxiety or shyness, the transition to an unstructured social environment can be challenging. Most first-year college students feel some degree of nervousness and excitement at the thought of meeting new people. Push yourself to work through any social nervousness you may have.

Real Life Scenario

Monique is a college freshman who spends many hours each night in her dorm room doing homework. She feels homesick, stays in her room, and frequently calls her parents and friends from home. She is nervous about meeting new people and hasn't made any new friends yet at college. One evening her Resident Assistant knocks on her door to say hello. The RA lets Monique know that all of the rooms on the floor of her residence hall are having an ice cream social later that night. At the event, first year students who live in Monique's residence hall will make ice cream sundaes and get to know each other. The RA asks Monique if she wants to attend.

What is a possible outcome if Monique <u>doesn't</u> attend the ice cream social?
_____
_____

What is a possible outcome if Monique <u>does</u> attend the ice cream social?
_____
_____

What would YOU do in this situation if you were Monique? Why?
_____
_____

23 EXERCISE
Student Tip: Know your learning style

From the Book

We all have qualities that make us unique such as our interests, personality and learning style. Some students prefer to learn in the morning while others learn better in the afternoon or evening. Knowing your learning style and preferences are important things to know about yourself as a student. Once you understand your learning style you can make decisions to help you be more successful throughout college.

Think About It

There are three types of learning styles; visual, auditory and kinesthetic. Everyone has a mixture of these learning styles but we each tend to learn best with primarily one of these methods. Think about the classes you have done well in and enjoyed. Did the teacher's teaching style play into your success in that class?

Consider the three learning styles below and determine which one tends to help you retain information most easily:

Auditory Learner
Do you enjoy learning from teachers who lecture and tell stories? If you enjoy learning by listening, then you may be an auditory learner.

Visual Learner
Do you enjoy teachers who use videos, PowerPoint presentations, and write notes & diagrams on the board? If so, you may be a visual learner.

Kinesthetic Learner
Do you enjoy learning in classes that allow you to participate in hands-on activities in class? If this describes how you learn best, you may be a kinesthetic learner.

Which of these learning styles describes how you learn best? Can you provide an example?

_____
_____
_____
_____

24 EXERCISE

Student Tip: Speaking up for yourself is important

From the Book

In college, if you don't say anything about a problem, the staff and professors will assume that you have everything under control. If you are having trouble with anything (classes, roommate, mental health, etc.), **YOU** need to speak up. In college, no one will know your likes, dislikes, learning style, or how your teachers helped you learn and be successful previously. **YOU** need to talk about these topics – your parents can't talk to the college academic staff like they could when you were in high school, and it isn't their responsibility.

Think About It

Who usually speaks up for you now when you need help or have a question in school – is it you? Is it your parents? Who usually speaks up for you when you need help or have a question about extracurricular activities outside of school (sports team, band or chorus, drama club, your job, volunteer opportunity, etc.)?

Use the space below to depict a recent situation when you needed to ask for help or had a question. Please note **WHO** asked for help or spoke up in that scenario.

{ }

If **YOU** were the person who asked for help in the scenario above, write one positive skill that you used when you asked for help. If someone else spoke up for you (such as a parent), write one way that you can begin to work on being more confident to speak up for yourself in college:

_____
_____

24

25 EXERCISE

Student Tip: Remember to keep your devices charged

From the Book

Without electricity, your electrical appliances are useless. If you forget to charge your battery-powered devices, they won't be available when you need them to take notes in class, type homework assignments, or access a textbook online. It's VERY important to remember to charge the battery-powered devices, such as your phone, computer, or tablet you will need the next day.

Think About It

You are likely using devices both at home and at school that need to be charged. How do you remember to charge these devices? Do you plug them in at a certain time of day or maybe always in the same location? Consider how many charging cords you require for all of your different devices (plus 1 or 2 backups— the Power of Multiples!).

On the phone screen to the left, list the devices that you plan to take to college that need to be regularly charged

How do you remember to charge your devices? Do you have a specific charging location or routine?

_____
_____
_____

Considering the devices you listed, write down the number of charging and power extension cords you will need to pack.

Check your college's residence life policy for info on approved power strips and extension cords

EXERCISE 26

Student Tip: Understand how your disability affects you

From the Book

Knowing what your disability is, and understanding how it affects you, are two different things. The best way to understand your disability is to ask your parents, high school teachers, school counselor or coach. These people can help you think about the ways your disability may affect you in college. It might be hard for you, alone, to imagine how your disability will affect you in that new setting. Understanding your disability can help you self-advocate and ask for tools to help you be successful.

Think About It

Knowing how your disability affects you in high school can help you prepare for college. You will be ahead of the game if you have already thought about the questions below.

How could your disability or medical condition affect <u>living on campus</u> at college?

_____
_____
_____

How could your disability or medical condition affect you <u>academically</u> at college?

_____
_____
_____

How could your disability or medical condition affect you socially (making friendships, getting along with your roommate, at social events) at college?

_____
_____
_____

27 EXERCISE

Student Tip: If you need accommodations, ask for them

From the Book

College is a brand new environment where every new student starts over with a clean slate. You know nothing about the other students and professors, and they know nothing about you. This means that no one will know if you have a learning disability, medical condition, or mental health condition unless you tell them. It's up to YOU to ask for the tools that will help you be successful in class, on campus, etc. Tools that you use to be successful because of your disability are called accommodations, and the staff in the Accessibility Office can assist you in determining what options are available.

Think About It

In high school, accommodations are typically built into students' schedules so students don't need to ask for them. Ideally, students have been involved in the IEP/504 process in high school so they know the accommodations they are receiving. This is a great time to think about the types of support you may already have and the support you will need in college.

Did you receive academic accommodations in high school?

If you answered yes, write the accommodations you received in the space below. If you answered no, can you think of any accommodations that may be helpful in your future college classes or college experience?

_____
_____
_____
_____
_____
_____

If you answered 'I'm not sure', this is a good opportunity to talk with your family or teachers. They can share with you whether or not you are receiving accommodations in high school and, if you are, they can identify the types of support you have in place.

28 EXERCISE

Student Tip: Visit the campus Accessibility Office - It's a great resource!

From the Book

By law, every college and university is required to provide reasonable accommodations for students with diagnosed disabilities. The staff in the Accessibility Office are there to provide you with accommodations to help you access your class content. This office is not a tutoring center – they will not help you with your homework, but they will talk with you about how your disability affects you in the classroom, in residence halls, etc., review documents that you have that verify your disability, help you solve conflicts you might be having with your professors because of your disability, and talk with you about assistive technology that could help you in the classroom.

1. Go to your college's website.
2. Find the Accessibility Office, Disability Services or Academic Support section of the website.
3. Fill the spaces below with the helpful information you find.

Where is the Accessibility Office Located?

Building: _____

Room Number: _____

Notes: _____

When is the Office Open to Students?

Days: _____

Times: _____

Notes: _____

List the Names of the Staff Who Work There

_____
_____
_____
_____

Ways to Contact the Accessibility Office

Email: _____

Phone: _____

Website: _____

Social Media: _____

29 EXERCISE

Student Tip: Be independent, but don't be too proud to ask for help

From the Book

Being independent is important. However, sometimes students are so determined to "do college on their own" that they refuse to ask for help. Being independent is a great quality, but if you start to struggle, there is nothing wrong with reaching out for help. If you're struggling in an area that is affected by your disability, visit the Accessibility Office. Your Academic Advisor is another person on campus who is a great resource to seek out when you need help. They can assist you you in resolving academic issues and connect you with other campus resources that can help if you are struggling in other areas.

Real Life Scenario

Emma is a college freshman who lived with depression throughout high school. She met with a counselor once a week in high school, but decided to stop seeing a counselor in college because she feels like she is ready to try college on her own. Emma has a successful first two weeks of college! In mid-September she starts to feel overwhelmed by her coursework and has some small arguments with her roommate. Emma notices that she is spending more time alone in her room and has trouble sleeping. When her parents call, Emma doesn't want to disappoint them so she tells them that everything is fine. By the end of September Emma is completely overwhelmed, oversleeping and missing classes, and not eating three meals a day. Emma thinks the campus counselor won't understand what she is going through so she doesn't want to ask for help.

✎ What advice would you give to Emma?

_____
_____
_____
_____

✎ Who are some of the people that Emma could go to for help (emotional or academic)?

_____
_____
_____

EXERCISE 30

Student Tip: Don't guess how well you're doing in your classes – Find out!

From the Book

College professors typically don't keep their students informed of their class grades. It's up to YOU to find out. At any point in the semester, you should know the grade you are earning. If you don't know your grade, find out. Colleges provide midterm grades and final grades, and sometimes an early academic report three to four weeks into the semester. The easiest way to find out your grades at any time in the semester is to look on your college's online management system or portal. If you wait until the college provides you with a report, it may be too late to improve your grades by the end of the semester.

Real Life Scenario

Michael is an avid gamer who enjoys playing video games at home and online with friends. At the beginning of college, Michael meets many new friends who enjoy playing video games too! Michael and his friends play video games until 2:00 a.m. or 3:00 a.m. every night and, although he is tired, Michael attends every class. However, Michael doesn't spend any time doing homework. In high school, Michael's teachers would remind him to turn in missing assignments. In college, none of his professors have approached him about his missing homework so Michael assumes he is doing well in his courses. When midterm grades are entered by professors in October, Michael is shocked to see four Fs! Michael didn't realize he was failing his classes and is upset that no one told him.

Why do you think Michael is failing his classes?
_____
_____
_____
_____

What advice do you have for Michael?
_____
_____
_____
_____

Identify two ways that Michael could have discovered how he was doing in his classes during the semester

1. _____

2. _____

Academic & Executive Functioning Skill-Building

EXCLUSIVE WORKBOOK ACTIVITY:
Assignment Planning

Can you help these students plan how to reach their goals? Draw a star in the box of the day when the task is due or happening then write each activity on the day of the week where you think it best fits.

Example Scenario: Sam has a writing assignment due on Friday. Today is Monday. They are writing about seals. They need to research seals on the computer, write an outline for their paper, and write their paper to turn in to their teacher by Friday.

Directions: Write these steps in the table below when you think Sam should complete each step

Monday	Tuesday	Wednesday	Thursday	Friday
Research seals on the computer	Write an Outline	Write Their Paper		Writing Assignment Due ★

Can you think of another way that Sam can plan their week and complete their writing assignment by Friday? Try the activity again, but this time write the activities on different days of the week.

Monday	Tuesday	Wednesday	Thursday	Friday
				Writing Assignment Due ★

- -

Scenario: Miguel's family is planning a trip to New York City on Friday. Today is Tuesday. Miguel's family needs to research fun things to do in New York City, buy tickets for the museum, go to the gas station so they have a full tank of gas, and buy a pair of new sneakers for Miguel so he can walk around the city in style.

Directions: Can you write these steps out in the table below for when you think Miguel's family should complete each step?

Monday	Tuesday	Wednesday	Thursday	Friday

Can you think of another way that Miguel's family can complete these tasks so they are ready to travel to New York City on Friday?

Monday	Tuesday	Wednesday	Thursday	Friday

EXCLUSIVE WORKBOOK ACTIVITY:
Task Initiation & Doing Things We Don't Want To

Read the list of activities below and use the rating scale to circle how much you WANT or DON'T WANT to do the activities. Once you've rated each activity, identify the 2 activities that you DON'T WANT to do the most (the activities where you circled 1 or 2). Write them in the space near the bottom of this page. Then identify 1 thing you could do to try to improve your ability to start this activity - even though you don't want to!

1 = I really don't want to do this   3 = I don't mind doing this   5 = I like to do this

Activity: Your Rating:

Activity	Rating
Make My Bed	1 2 3 4 5
Go Shopping	1 2 3 4 5
Go to the Beach	1 2 3 4 5
Play Basketball	1 2 3 4 5
Do Math Homework	1 2 3 4 5
Do Science Homework	1 2 3 4 5
Write a Poem	1 2 3 4 5
Listen to Music	1 2 3 4 5
Read a Book	1 2 3 4 5
Hang out with Friends	1 2 3 4 5

Choose two activities from the list you don't want to do and come up with ways you could help yourself to initiate this activity

1. _____

2. _____

EXCLUSIVE WORKBOOK ACTIVITY:
Scheduling & Morning Routine

> Lana has an Intro to Criminal Justice class on Tuesday & Friday morning at 9:00 a.m. She likes to go to the fitness center on campus for a yoga class on Friday mornings at 7:30 a.m. She uses a campus meal plan to eat breakfast in the dining hall and brings a granola bar and juice with her on mornings when she doesn't have time to eat breakfast. The dining hall and fitness center are both about a 15 minute walk from her residence hall.

On Tuesday, Lana eats breakfast at 8:15 a.m. before class. What time should she wake up to be at the dining hall by 8:15 a.m.? →

On Friday, what time should Lana wake up to arrive at the yoga class on time? →

On Friday, do you think Lana has time to eat breakfast? If so, what time(s) fit into her schedule? →

What are some delays or distractions that Lana could experience that might keep her from sticking to their schedule and showing up on time?

💬 Conversation Starters for Families

1. Does your student have a morning routine at home? If so, how much of the morning routine is initiated by your student versus prompted by others? How can you begin to give independence to your student?

2. How will your student ensure they can wake up on time for class in college? Alarm clock, cell phone alarm, etc?

3. Alarm clocks (or lack thereof) can affect college roommates when one roommate needs to wake up for a class and the other roommate does not. Talk about this situation and potential roommate conflict before leaving for college.

EXCLUSIVE WORKBOOK ACTIVITY:
Textbook Options & Preferences

Before the beginning of each course, professors will identify if you need to purchase a textbook for their class. Textbooks are usually in stock at the bookstore on campus. You can also purchase new, used or even rent textbooks online. Did you know that textbooks come in different formats? You can purchase a physical textbook, an electronic textbook, or an audio textbook. You may not have all of these choices in high school, but if you did have a choice, which type of textbook would you prefer? List your personal pros and cons for each textbook type below.

Physical Textbook
Do you like holding the textbook in your hands, highlighting, writing on the pages, and turning the pages?

Pros _____ **Cons** _____

Electronic Textbook
Do you like reading the words on the computer or tablet screen? Do you prefer having textbooks accessible on your device at any time?

Pros _____ **Cons** _____

Audio Textbook
Do you prefer having audio textbooks that can be read aloud on your computer or device?

Pros _____ **Cons** _____

💬 Conversation Starters for Families
Think about these options and which one will help your student understand and remember the material they are learning. Some students even choose more than one option and purchase a physical textbook AND an electronic textbook. In college, the choice is yours!

EXCLUSIVE WORKBOOK ACTIVITY:
Express Yourself: Procrastination

Prompt: What does procrastination feel like?

Draw pictures, shapes or words in the space below

EXCLUSIVE WORKBOOK ACTIVITY:
College Writing Exercise

Write a paragraph response to the following sentence starters:

Name:
Class:
Date:

One of my strengths that I will bring to college is...

One of my skills that I can improve before going to college is...

A question I have about college is...

EXCLUSIVE WORKBOOK ACTIVITY:
High School vs. College

HIGH SCHOOL	COLLEGE
Teachers remind students of missing assignments	Professors likely will not remind students of upcoming due dates or missing work
Teachers often write information on the board as a summary of notes.	Professors may lecture non-stop, expecting students to take notes on what they identify are important points.
Teachers are often available for conversation before, during, or after class to answer student questions.	If students have questions, professors expect, and want, the student to attend their scheduled office hours.
Write your own idea here:	**Write your own idea here:**
Write your own idea here:	**Write your own idea here:**

EXCLUSIVE WORKBOOK ACTIVITY:
Real-World Time Management & Organizational Scenarios

Topic Information

Time management and organization are two important skills that can help you manage your schedule and responsibilities in college. Read the scenarios below and make a plan to complete each goal, project or scenario. Consider breaking down larger assignments and using a calendar, planner or app to help you stay on track and not procrastinate until the night before it is due.

SCENARIO #1: You are given a homework assignment during class on Thursday. The assignment is to read an article distributed in class, summarize it and then write your response in 1.5 pages. The assignment should be completed by Monday's class. Use the template below to outline the steps you would take to complete the assignment.

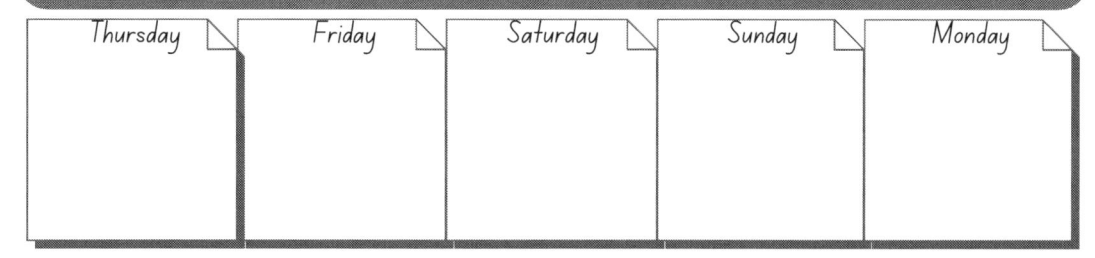

Thursday	Friday	Saturday	Sunday	Monday

SCENARIO #2: You are assigned a group project in class on Monday. You need to meet with your group and make a PowerPoint presentation that is due in class on Friday. Everyone in your group needs to contribute to the group project by making 2 slides each. There are 4 members in each group (3 classmates and you). Use the template below to outline the steps you would take to complete the assignment.

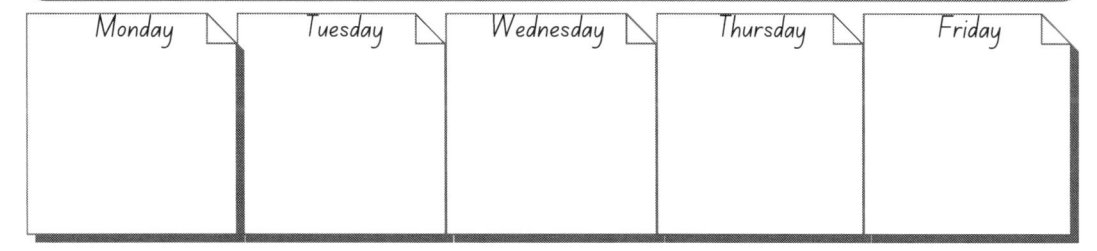

Monday	Tuesday	Wednesday	Thursday	Friday

SCENARIO #3: You've finalized your fall class schedule with your Academic Advisor and classes start Monday. Your semester starts the next week on Monday. Identify 3 tasks you could do to help you prepare for your first day of classes.

1. _____   2. _____   3. _____

EXCLUSIVE WORKBOOK ACTIVITY:
It's Time To Get Organized!

Topic Information

Organization of your school supplies and papers is important. Equally as important is the organizational system on your computer. Think about your current organizational system for your papers, notes and assignments and follow prompts below.

How do you organize your school work and tangible belongings currently?

How do you organize your electronic files on the computer/Google Drive currently?

Identify one or two organization tasks that you can tackle this week to help your tangible belongings or computer files become more organized and how you plan to accomplish this goal.

Pro Tip: As soon as you receive your semester schedule you should create folders on your computer for each course you are taking. This is where you should put all class notes, syllabi, and assignments. Then be sure to label your files in each folder by including the course name. For example: Psychology - Fall 21

EXCLUSIVE WORKBOOK ACTIVITY:
Your Phone As A Support Resource

Topic Information

College can be tough, but there's an app for that - actually there are a lot of apps! The best apps for college students are the ones that can simplify your life and make your time in school more enjoyable. Your mobile device could become one of your most-used school supplies. There are apps that can help you meet your deadlines, study more efficiently, stay connected to the people who matter most, and manage many aspects of your college experience. When thinking about which apps to add to your mobile device, check first to see if your college has its own app. Depending on the capabilities of your school's app, you may be able to access calendars, courses, events, and other important information that keeps you more connected to your campus.

First, identify a skill that you would like to improve or manage better at college (i.e. time management, campus involvement scheduling, note taking, etc.)

Activity

Use the internet or the App/Play store to research apps that might help you with this particular skill. On the phone screen to the left, list the helpful resources you find.

Example: If you experience anxiety, you can look in the App store for apps that offer guided meditation, relaxing sounds, or positive messages delivered to your phone every day.

EXCLUSIVE WORKBOOK ACTIVITY:
Time Waster Assessment

Topic Information

Have you ever felt like time was passing quickly and you lost an hour? Do you ever wonder where the time goes? To find out where YOUR time goes, check off the time wasters that apply to you.

Time Wasters **You Have** Control Over

- ☐ Talking on the phone with friends
- ☐ Scrolling through videos
- ☐ Watching movies/TV shows
- ☐ Listening to music
- ☐ Checking email
- ☐ Daydreaming
- ☐ Worrying
- ☐ Making avoidable mistakes
- ☐ Poor study skills
- ☐ Low concentration
- ☐ Lack of planning
- ☐ Playing computer or video games
- ☐ Consuming alcohol or drugs
- ☐ Excessive worrying about homework
- ☐ Indecision about making choices

Time Wasters **You Don't Have** Control Over

- ☐ Phone interruptions
- ☐ Music/Noise in the area
- ☐ Delays/Waiting
- ☐ Roommate problems
- ☐ Unclear assignments
- ☐ Too many demands
- ☐ Other people's problems/drama
- ☐ Illness
- ☐ Emergencies
- ☐ Family
- ☐ Meetings
- ☐ Traffic
- ☐ Internet outage
- ☐ Technology/Device failure
- ☐ Job

Time wasters that affect me the most are...

_____
_____
_____

Strategies I can use to reduce the time I waste are...

_____
_____
_____

EXCLUSIVE WORKBOOK ACTIVITY:
Time Management, Organization & Scheduling

Topic Information

Time management and organization are two important skills that can help you manage your schedule and responsibilities in college. Every semester, once you register for your new classes you should create a visual schedule. Visual, week-at-a glance, schedules can help you remember the days and times of classes, appointments, meetings with friends, personal responsibilities, etc. "Keeping it all in your head" usually doesn't work in college.

Use the blank schedule below to create a visual schedule of your week right now. Use a different color for each class, each appointment, etc.

Quick Tip: Use the template in the back of this workbook when you go to college to make a new schedule every semester.

	Monday	Tuesday	Wednesday	Thursday	Friday	Sat/Sun
8:00						
9:00						
10:00						
11:00						
12:00						
1:00						
2:00						
3:00						
4:00						
5:00						

EXCLUSIVE WORKBOOK ACTIVITY:
Breaking Down Large Projects - Part One

Topic Information

College professors will assign large assignments/projects, provide the due date, and they may not mention the project again. It will be up to you to manage your time and complete the project by the due date without waiting until the last minute.

Activity: Read the scenario below. Break down the large project into 5 smaller steps. Write the 5 smaller steps in the calendar on the days when you would complete them.

SCENARIO: Today is October 2nd. Your psychology professor asks you to read chapters 1, 2, 3, 4 and 5 in your textbook. You are also required to create a PowerPoint presentation with at least 15 slides on a topic of your choice from one of the chapters. You will submit your PowerPoint and give a presentation in class about the topic you chose.
This project is due on October 25th.

1	2	3	4	5	6	7
8	9	10	11	12	13	14
15	16	17	18	19	20	21
22	23	24	25	26	27	28
29	30	31				

EXCLUSIVE WORKBOOK ACTIVITY:
Breaking Down Large Projects - Part Two

Topic Information

College professors will assign large assignments/projects, provide the due date, and they may not mention the project again. It will be up to you to manage your time and complete the project by the due date without saving it to the last minute.

Activity: Read the scenario below. Break down the large project into 5 smaller steps. Write the 5 small steps in the calendar on the days when you would complete them.

SCENARIO: Today is March 4th. Your Intro to College Writing professor asks you to choose a controversial current events topic, choose one perspective of the issue, find two research articles that support your point and write a four page essay. The final essay is due on March 27th.

1	2	3	4	5	6	7
8	9	10	11	12	13	14
15	16	17	18	19	20	21
22	23	24	25	26	27	28
29	30	31				

EXCLUSIVE WORKBOOK ACTIVITY:
Breaking Down Large Projects - Part Three

Topic Information

College professors will assign large assignments/projects, provide the due date, and they may not mention the project again. It will be up to you to manage your time and complete the project by the due date without saving it to the last minute.

Activity: Read the scenario below. Break down the large project into 5 smaller steps. Write the 5 small steps in the calendar on the days when you would complete them.

SCENARIO: Today is January 1st and Emily has two projects due on January 15th - her college application and a science group lab report. Emily is applying to Crashman College for Aeronautics and needs to write her Common App essay, ask her school counselor for a letter of recommendation, and ask her grandmother for the fifty dollar college application fee. She needs to submit all three application materials by January 15th.

She also has a science group presentation to finish. Her science teacher split the class into small groups of four students and each group tested two samples of water from the small pond on the high school campus. Each group needs to create a PowerPoint presentation of their water sample findings to present to the class. Each group must also meet one time outside of class (in person or virtually) to decide who will speak during the class presentation. The group slideshow needs to be submitted to the teacher at least one day before their presentation. The class presentation is due January 15th.

1	2	3	4	5	6	7
8	9	10	11	12	13	14
15	16	17	18	19	20	21
22	23	24	25	26	27	28
29	30	31				

EXCLUSIVE WORKBOOK ACTIVITY:
Self-Advocacy & Time Management Scenarios

Topic Information

Speaking up for things you need is an important skill. Campus staff assume no news is good news. If they don't hear from you they assume you are doing well. Time management is also a skill that is completely on you.

Activity: Read the scenarios below and shade the circle that describes the action you are most likely to do.

SCENARIO #1
Your teacher gives you a difficult assignment and there are some things you don't understand. Are you most likely to:
- ○ Ask your teacher for help
- ○ Ask a friend for help
- ○ Ask your parent for help
- ○ Search on your own to find answers

SCENARIO #2
You have a busy schedule with school, a sports team and a part-time job giving tours for the Admissions Office. Are you most likely to:
- ○ Set aside 1 hour each day to study
- ○ Study when you get the chance
- ○ Study only the night before a test
- ○ Create a weekly schedule based on your assignments when you can study

SCENARIO #3
You are allergic to tree nuts & shellfish and need to request dietary accommodations with the Accessibility Office. Are you most likely to:
- ○ Visit the office as soon as you are accepted to the college
- ○ Ask your parents to contact the office because they are better at advocating than you
- ○ Avoid contacting the office because you don't want to seem pushy

SCENARIO #4
Imagine your fall semester starts in two days and you just bought your textbooks. Are you most likely to:
- ○ Flip through the textbooks & set them aside
- ○ Start reading the first chapter
- ○ Look through the textbooks to find chapter headings
- ○ Put the textbooks in a drawer until you're given your first assignment

EXCLUSIVE WORKBOOK ACTIVITY:
Procrastination at College

Don't put this activity off until tomorrow

Topic Information

Procrastination is a habit that plagues many students. Completing assignments at the last minute is not a good idea and can lead to stress and work that is less than your best. College will be full of stressors that will be out of your control, but procrastination stress can be avoided with a little planning, organization and self-discipline.

Real Life Scenario

Chen's alarm goes off at 7:00 a.m. and he hits the snooze button. When he opens his eyes Chen realizes it is 8:15 a.m. and his first class starts at 8:30 a.m. Chen jumps out of bed, gets dressed and grabs his backpack as he rushes out the door. In class, he realizes he forgot to grab the history essay due today sitting on the desk in his dorm room. Returning to his room after class, Chen is upset and decides to take a break by playing video games. Chen loses track of time and plays video games for two hours. He decides to start on his psychology homework and realizes he forgot the password to log in to his college email account where his professor sent the assignment directions. Frustrated again, Chen texts his teammates to make plans for dinner then walks to the dining hall. After dinner Chen has forty-five minutes before his soccer practice begins and he wants to start his math homework but doesn't think he has enough time. After soccer practice Chen returns to his room and plays video games again to relax. He realizes it's now midnight and he hasn't completed any homework. He drinks an energy drink, gets a burst of energy and stays up doing homework until 3:00 a.m. He sets his alarm for 7:00 a.m. the next morning.

Can you relate to Chen's story? Why or why not?
_____
_____

What are suggestions you have for Chen to help with his time management?
_____
_____

EXCLUSIVE WORKBOOK ACTIVITY:
Prioritizing College Assignments – Part One

Topic Information

You will have at least four or more courses each semester in college. Each course instructor will assign their own individual assignments and projects which will have separate due dates. If you have four or more assignments due each week how do you prioritize which assignments to complete first? How do you know which assignments are the most important?

Activity: Look at the real-world scenarios below and indicate with an "X" which assignment you would do first.

To Do List
- [ ] Read a History article and write a response essay due on Thursday
- [ ] Read Psychology chapter 3 due on Friday

To Do List
- [ ] Sports Management reading quiz worth 10% of your overall grade
- [ ] College Writing first essay draft worth 15% of your overall grade

To Do List
- [ ] Marine Ecology lab worksheet due on Tuesday & is worth 5% of your overall grade
- [ ] Marine Ecology chapter 1, 2, 3 exam is on Friday & worth 25% of your overall grade

To Do List
- [ ] Intro to Film Studies has a film to watch & a 2 page essay response is due on Friday
- [ ] Political Science chapters 5, 6, 7, 8 exam is due on Friday

⚠ Quick Tip

There are two main ways to prioritize assignments:
ONE: Complete assignments that are due soonest first
TWO: Complete assignments that are worth the most points (or largest percentage) first

EXCLUSIVE WORKBOOK ACTIVITY:
Prioritizing College Assignments - Part Two

Topic Information

You will have at least 4 or more courses each semester in college. Each course instructor will assign their own individual assignments and projects which will have separate due dates. If you have 4 or more assignments due each week how do you prioritize which assignments to complete first? How do you know which assignments are the most important?

Activity: Look at the real-world scenarios below and indicate with an "X" which assignment you would prioritize to do first.

To Do List
- [ ] Watch a documentary for World Religion class and answer given questions by Friday
- [ ] Read Hospitality & Tourism textbook chapters 10 & 11 due on Wednesday

To Do List
- [ ] Sports Management online discussion board post worth 5% of your overall grade
- [ ] Business marketing plan draft worth 10% of your overall grade

To Do List
- [ ] Effective Communication course autobiography oral presentation is due on Wednesday
- [ ] Marine Ecology chapters 5, 6, 7, 8 exam is on Friday
- [ ] Digital Photography read chapter 3 and take 20 pictures due on Wed.

To Do List
- [ ] Read a Creative Writing article and a 2 page essay is due on Thursday worth 20% of your overall grade
- [ ] History II chapters 10, 11, 12 exam on Friday worth 35% of your grade
- [ ] 40 Accounting problems due Friday worth 5% of our overall grade

Quick Tip

There are 2 main ways to prioritize assignments.
ONE: Complete assignments that are due soonest first
TWO: Complete assignments that are worth the most points (or largest percentage)

Self-Awareness, Self-Advocacy, Connecting to Campus Resources & Communication Skill-Building

EXCLUSIVE WORKBOOK ACTIVITY:
Campus Health & Wellness

1. Go to your college's website.
2. Find the Student Life or Campus Life section of the website.
3. Search for the various Health & Wellness services that are offered on campus. Search for physical health services (walk-in clinic, nurse/doctor on staff) and mental health supports (counseling center, support groups, 24-hour helplines).

List the physical health services listed on the website:

After doing research, do you have any remaining questions about physical health services on campus?

List the mental health services listed on the website:

After doing research, do you have any remaining questions about mental health services on campus?

EXCLUSIVE WORKBOOK ACTIVITY:
Roommate Communication

Communicating your preferences is critical. When it comes to key issues like sleeping, studying, and socializing, it's wise to talk about these issues with your roommate from the beginning of the semester. Having a roommate means that you will need to communicate with your roommate about many different situations. How would you start a conversation with your roommate in these scenarios?

Scenario	Your Response
Your roommate stays up late playing music and watching movies and you can't sleep.	
Your roommate uses your belongings without asking.	
Your roommate wants to hang out with you all the time but you need some space and want to hang out with other friends.	
Your roommate doesn't clean the room or empty the garbage can.	
Your roommate's dirty clothes are on your side of the room.	
Your roommate orders takeout food and leaves the pizza boxes and takeout containers in the overflowing garbage.	
Your roommate leaves the dorm room unlocked but you feel strongly that you want the room locked	

Conversation Starters for Families

1. When living with another person, conflicts are bound to happen. It is best for students to think about how they could solve potential conflicts before they happen when emotions may be running high.

2. Proactively thinking about possible roommate scenarios is important particularly for students who may not have shared a room before.

EXCLUSIVE WORKBOOK ACTIVITY:
Questions to Ask Campus Accessibility Offices

1. Go to your college's website.
2. Find the Accessibility Office webpage.
3. Search for the information to answer the questions below.

Name of College:
Name of Director of Accessibility Office:
Contact Info:

How many staff (full-time, part-time, peer mentors) work in the Accessibility Office?

Are there deadlines or important dates that students need to know in order to request accommodations (for classroom or testing purposes)?

Does the Accessibility Office offer fee-based systems of tiered supports such as academic coaching, executive functioning support, autism social supports, etc.?

What is the college's process for requesting accommodations? Can students complete the process online or do students need to visit the Accessibility Office in person? How are faculty notified of student accommodations, online or in person?

What methods does the Accessibility Office use to communicate with students? Email, text, college online learning management system (Blackboard, Canvas, etc.)?

EXCLUSIVE WORKBOOK ACTIVITY:
Self-Reflection

> Going from high school to college is a BIG step, but one that will have a much smoother transition if you feel prepared, continue to ask questions and get support if you need it. College is going to be an incredible adventure, and you will learn so much both in and out of the classroom. Embrace the challenges, push yourself out of your comfort zone and try new things. Trust us, it will be worth it!

What I am most excited about:

What I am most anxious about:

What is one piece of advice I've been given about college:

EXCLUSIVE WORKBOOK ACTIVITY:
Self-Awareness

Self-awareness is an important skill that contributes to college success. Think about each area below and identify your strengths or areas you can improve to help you better understand your current skills. Remember, this is a snapshot in time and this simply reflects where your skills are right now. You can grow and change in any of these skill areas!

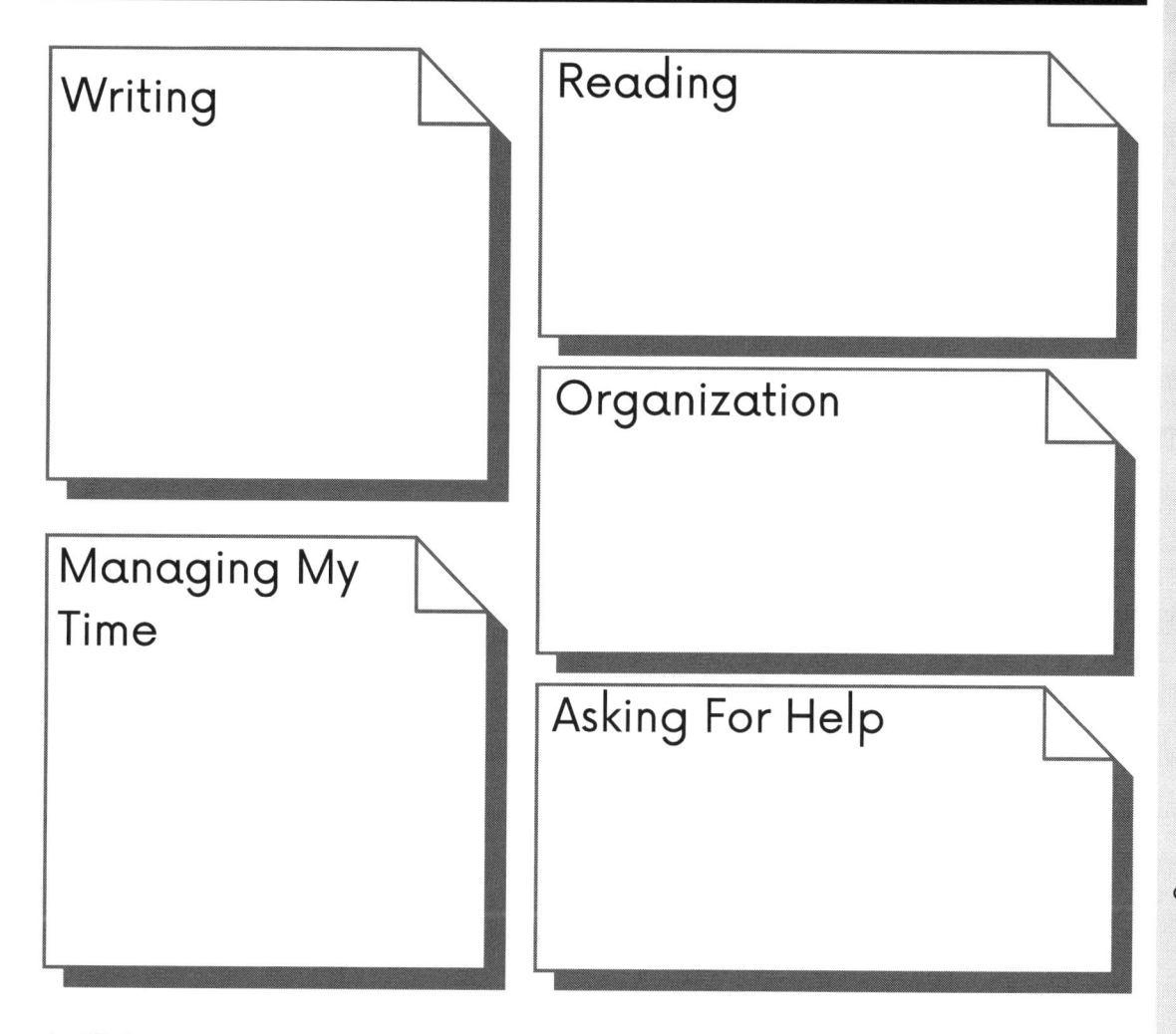

Writing

Reading

Organization

Managing My Time

Asking For Help

✎ Identify an area that you can start improving, and list one step you can take toward this goal:

EXCLUSIVE WORKBOOK ACTIVITY:
Healthy Transitions – Part One

> If you are currently working with a counselor for mental health support, it is important that you consider whether or not you will continue when you head off to college. Colleges have counseling centers or collaborations with local mental health professionals available to students. Research the resources available on your campus and fill out this worksheet in consultation with your clinician to prepare for your transition.

	Researched Information & Notes	Date Completed
Does the college have a counseling center?		
Where is the counseling center located?		
What are the counseling center's hours?		
Is there a cost associated with going to the counseling center?		
Is there a limit to how many sessions I can have at the counseling center?		
Does the counseling center or other campus department offer after-hours emergency help?		
Is medication management available at the counseling or health center?		
Are counseling services available during breaks and over summer when classes aren't in session?		
How do I make an appointment at the counseling center?		

EXCLUSIVE WORKBOOK ACTIVITY:
Healthy Transitions – Part Two

> If you are currently working with a counselor for mental health support, it is important that you consider if you will continue when you head off to college. Colleges have counseling centers or collaborations with local mental health professionals available to students. Research the resources available on your campus and fill out this worksheet in consultation with your clinician to prepare for your transition.

	Researched Information & Notes	Date Completed
What are the mental health resources available at my college or college's community?		
Have I considered whether or not I am close enough to home to continue treatment with my current provider?		
Have I considered the option of continuing with my current provider over Zoom/other technology?		
How will I get my medication on campus?		
Have I shared information about my condition with the college's counseling center		
If necessary, have I identified and been to see an off-campus provider?		
If applicable, have I found feasible transportation to appointments with my off-campus provider or have I found one within walking distance?		
If necessary, have I shared information about my condition between my current provider and my new off-campus provider?		

EXCLUSIVE WORKBOOK ACTIVITY:
Know Your Campus Mental Health Resources

Topic Information

Colleges and universities have many departments with services to support students' mental health. The resources and people in college that are available for you if you need to talk may have different names/titles than in high school. It is a great idea to find at least two people on campus who you feel comfortable talking to when things get hard or when you need help.

Activity: Complete this scavenger hunt for a college of your choice. Explore by clicking around the website or use the search bar on the website to find the contact information for the people and offices below that you can talk to if things get tough in college.

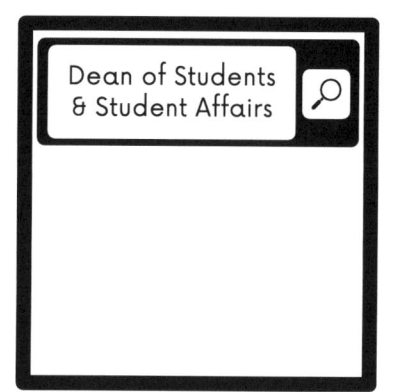

- Campus Counseling & Health Center
- Dean of Students & Student Affairs
- Academic Advising Staff
- Residence Hall Director & Resident Assistants
- Accessibility Office

EXCLUSIVE WORKBOOK ACTIVITY:
Self-Disclosure at College

> Self-disclosure is a personal decision. It can be helpful to discuss the decision to disclose a disability in college with your family, teachers, school counselors and other professionals. Ultimately the decision is up to you.
> The questions below will help you think about this important decision.

✏️ **What is the definition of self-disclosure?**

_____
_____
_____

What are possible benefits of self-disclosure at College?

What are possible drawbacks of self-disclosure at College?

✏️ **What are your thoughts about the decision to self-disclose at college?**

_____
_____
_____
_____
_____

EXCLUSIVE WORKBOOK ACTIVITY:
Understanding Your 504/IEP & Preparing for College

> Understanding the purpose of your 504/IEP, the accommodations included in it, and how they can help you to be successful in college is an important skill that can lead to your success! After completing this worksheet, you may want to bring it with you to your campus Accessibility Office to discuss the supports you may need in college.

✏️ I have a 504/IEP because:
_____
_____
_____

✏️ The accommodations in my 504/IEP plan are:
_____
_____
_____

✏️ This is how the accommodations in my 504/IEP plan help me:
_____
_____
_____

✏️ The accommodations I think will help me in college are:
_____
_____
_____

✏️ These are the questions I have about accommodations in college:
_____
_____
_____

EXCLUSIVE WORKBOOK ACTIVITY:
Self-Advocacy & Communicating With Professors

Topic Information

For students with disabilities, in order to receive accommodations in college you need to register with your campus' Accessibility Office and request accommodations that can help you be successful. Once approved, you will receive an Accommodation Letter stating the accommodations that you have been approved to use during that semester. The last step is notifying professors in each of your classes and sharing your accommodation letter with them typically by having a conversation with their professors (usually on the first or second day of class). Students may also be asked to email a copy of their accommodation letter to their professors.

Think About It

You may not have had to meet with a teacher to discuss your disability and accommodations in the past, but don't stress. Your professors have worked with countless students with a wide range of accommodation needs. Here are two examples of conversation starters that you can use, then see if you can create your own.

Example #1

"Hi Professor, my name is Ryan. This is my accommodation letter from the Accessibility Office. I need extra time when I take exams. Are you free now to talk with me for a few minutes about my accommodation?"

Example #2

"Professor, do you have office hours this week? I'd like to set up an appointment with you to talk about my disability and how it might affect me in your class."

Example #3

Example #4

EXCLUSIVE WORKBOOK ACTIVITY:
Conversations With Your Roommate - Part One

Topic Information

Having a roommate means that you will need to communicate with them in many different situations. Your Resident Assistants (RAs) in your residence hall are trained to help you and your roommate manage these conversations and help you get to a compromise if issues arise. Think about how you would start a conversation with your roommate if:

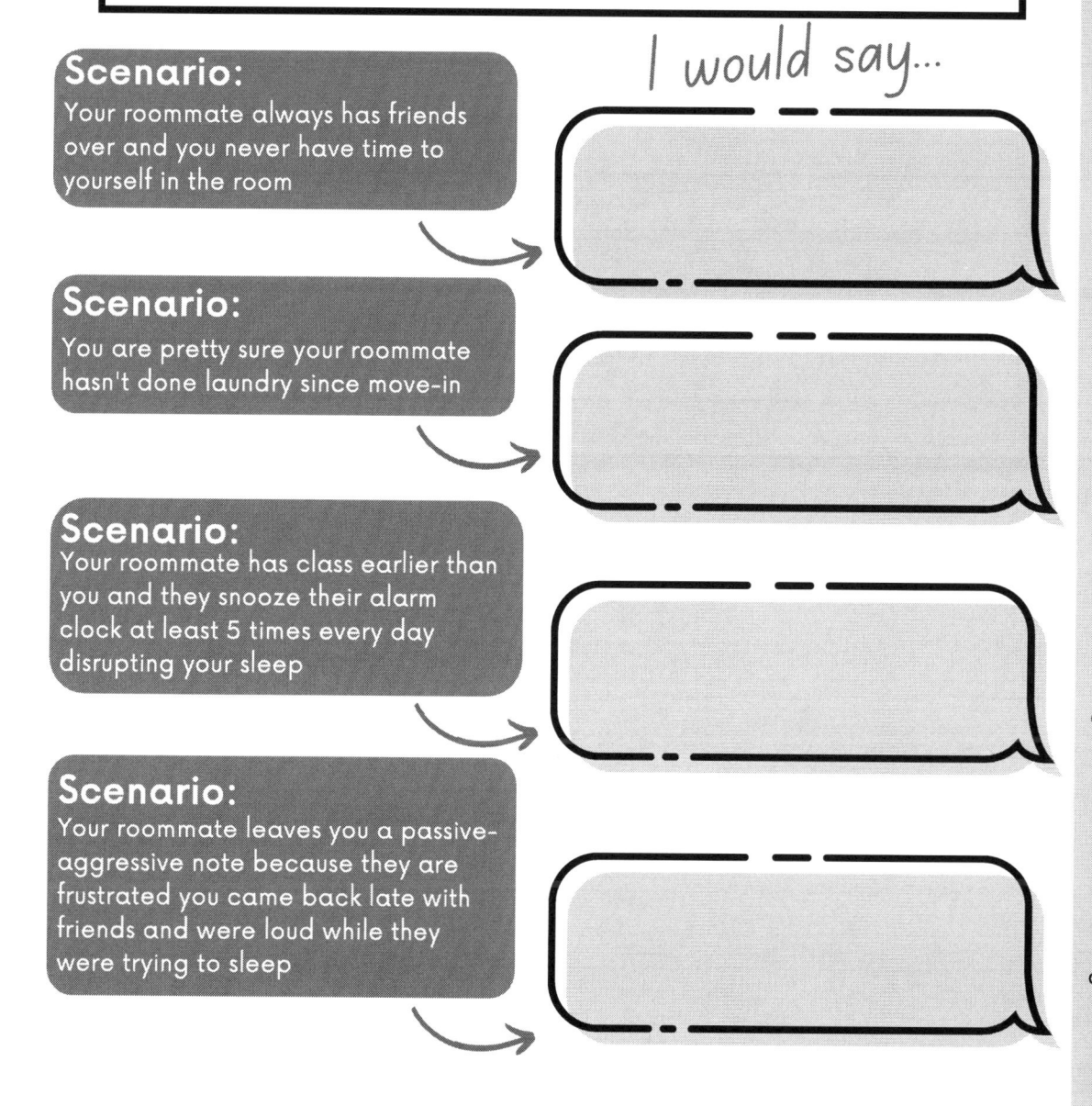

I would say...

Scenario: Your roommate always has friends over and you never have time to yourself in the room

Scenario: You are pretty sure your roommate hasn't done laundry since move-in

Scenario: Your roommate has class earlier than you and they snooze their alarm clock at least 5 times every day disrupting your sleep

Scenario: Your roommate leaves you a passive-aggressive note because they are frustrated you came back late with friends and were loud while they were trying to sleep

⚠️ <u>PRO TIP</u>: It may feel awkward, but these conversations are best to have face to face, not via text, social media, email, or handwritten notes... trust us on this one!

EXCLUSIVE WORKBOOK ACTIVITY:
Conversations With Your Roommate - Part Two

Topic Information

Having a roommate means that you will need to communicate with them in many different situations. Your Resident Assistants (RAs) in your residence hall are trained to help you and your roommate manage these conversations and help you get to a compromise if issues arise. Think about how you would start a conversation with your roommate if:

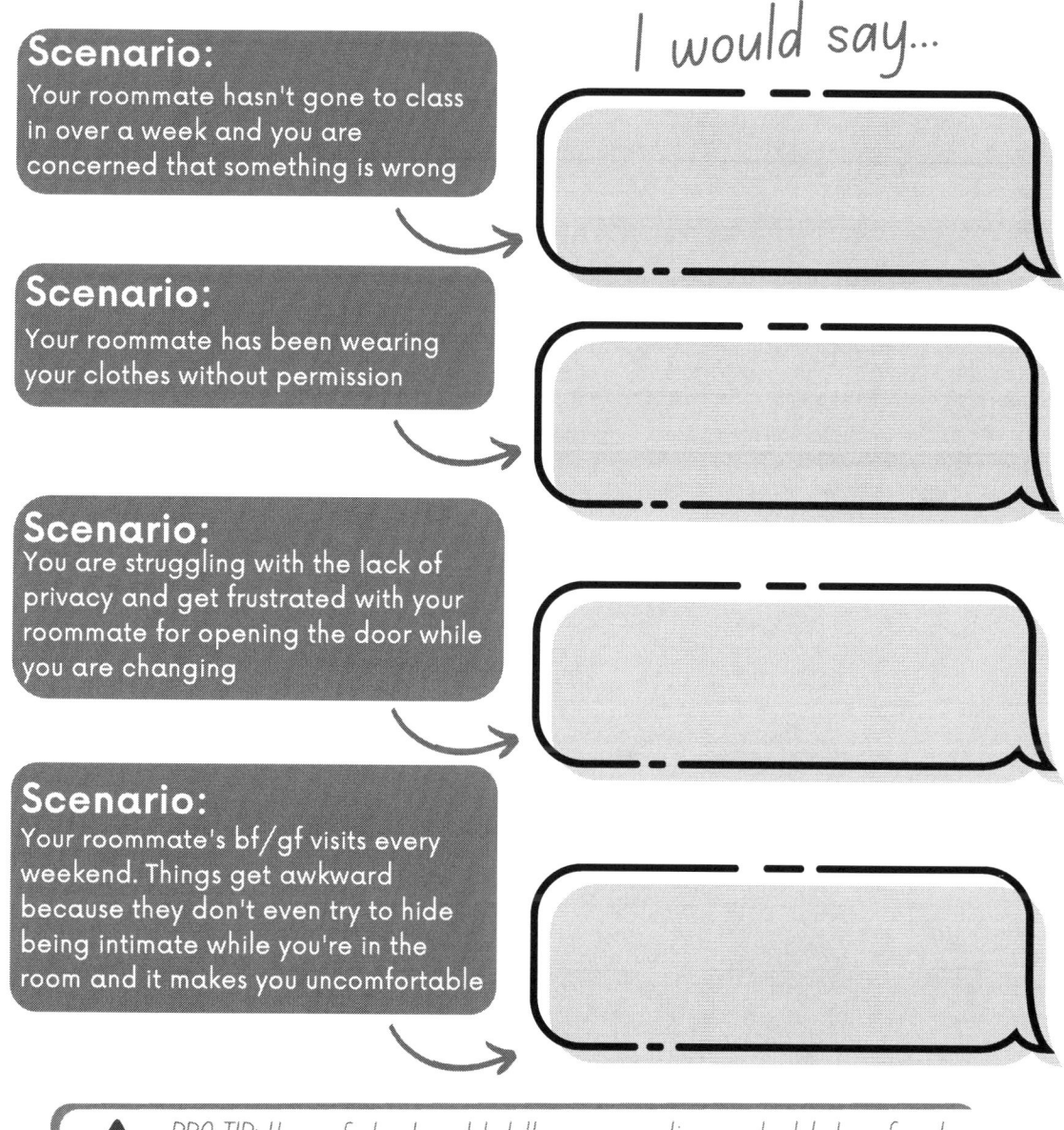

Scenario: Your roommate hasn't gone to class in over a week and you are concerned that something is wrong

I would say...

Scenario: Your roommate has been wearing your clothes without permission

Scenario: You are struggling with the lack of privacy and get frustrated with your roommate for opening the door while you are changing

Scenario: Your roommate's bf/gf visits every weekend. Things get awkward because they don't even try to hide being intimate while you're in the room and it makes you uncomfortable

⚠️ **PRO TIP:** It may feel awkward, but these conversations are best to have face to face, not via text, social media, email, or handwritten notes... trust us on this one!

EXCLUSIVE WORKBOOK ACTIVITY:
Express Yourself: Self Check-in

Prompt: Right now, how do you feel about college?

Draw pictures, shapes or words in the space below

EXCLUSIVE WORKBOOK ACTIVITY:
Talking About A Disability

Topic Information

In order to receive accommodations in college, you need to visit the Accessibility Office and provide evidence of a learning, medical, mental health or physical disability. Bringing documentation of a disability is one part of the process. Talking to an Accessibility Specialist about how your disability affects you is the second part.

It can be uncomfortable for some students to talk about their disability. Why do you think it could be uncomfortable?

If you have a disability or mental health condition, have you talked to people about your disability? If so, who have you talked to (teachers, coaches, family members, etc.)?

Do you know what types of documentation you have that mention your disability? If not, it's ok. This is a great time to ask your family or teachers about documentation. Remember in college **YOU** (not your parents or teachers) will need to provide documentation if you decide to request accommodations. List the documentation below that you have or might need to provide at college.

EXCLUSIVE WORKBOOK ACTIVITY:
Staying Physically Healthy at College

Topic Information

Your physical and mental health are important components of college success. It is hard to be academically successful when your body and/or mind aren't healthy. This activity will encourage you to reflect on ways you currently focus on fitness and encourage you to explore opportunities available on your college campus to keep the habits you have or try something new!

What do you do now to stay physically fit? For example, do you walk or run? Do you participate on a sport's team for your school or community? Do you do yoga, kayak, hike, or go to a gym? List the ways you take care of your body physically below:

Your campus likely has awesome recreation programs, intramural sports, wellness initiatives, fitness centers, group workouts and other resources for students generally at no additional cost. If you haven't yet looked into what your campus has to offer, check it out. Use the space below to write down activities that you may want to try when you get to campus as well as other ways you plan to stay physically fit at college.

EXCLUSIVE WORKBOOK ACTIVITY:
Connecting to Campus Outside of the Classroom

Topic Information

Students who get involved on campus outside of the classroom tend to have a higher GPA, faster degree completion, along with increased personal growth and cognitive development. Clubs, organizations, intermural sports and campus events are also great ways to meet people, build your community and create your unique college experience. Campuses typically coordinate Student Involvement Fairs near the start of the semester to showcase everything available for students on campus and in the local community.

1. Go to your college's website
2. Find the Student Life or Campus Activities section
3. Search for the various ways to get involved outside of the classroom

What did you find out? In the spaces below list clubs, groups or activities that you are interested in learning more about when you get to campus:

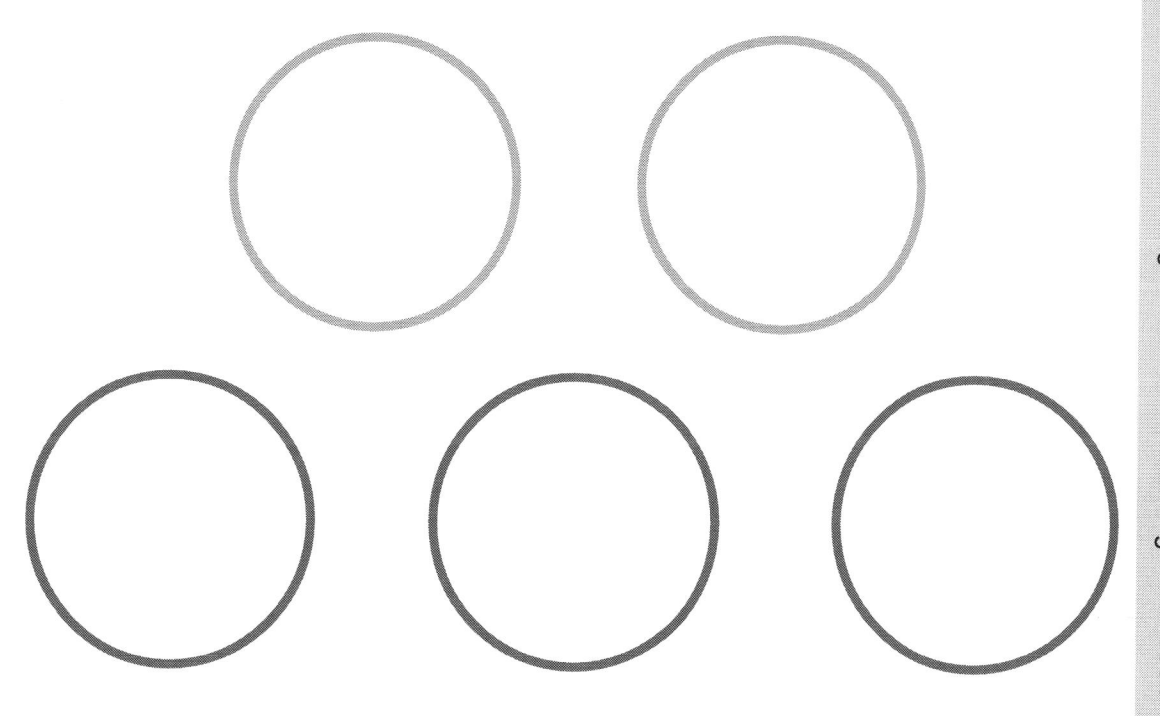

EXCLUSIVE WORKBOOK ACTIVITY:
Living On Your Own - The Good, The Bad & The Dirty

Topic Information

If you decide to live on campus, you will be living in a residence hall in a room by yourself or with a roommate. Similar to living at home, you will be responsible for keeping your space tidy and livable. Think about the chores you do at home to help keep your living space clean. For example, you might empty garbage cans, wipe or dust surfaces, vacuum the carpet, sweep the floor, etc.

Identify some of the chores you do at home and write them below	Daily	Weekly	Monthly
1	○	○	○
2	○	○	○
3	○	○	○
4	○	○	○

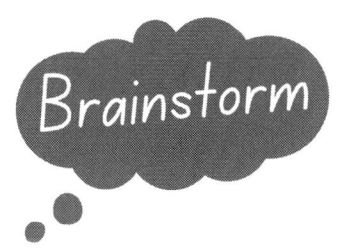

Brainstorm

Brainstorm chores that you imagine you will need to do in college to keep your living space clean and draw or write them below. Now think about sharing your space with a roommate. How can you share the responsibility of keeping your space clean?

EXCLUSIVE WORKBOOK ACTIVITY:
Self-Awareness & Bringing Your Strengths to College

Topic Information

All students have personal strengths including talents, character traits, knowledge and experiences that allow them to thrive in a learning environment. These are mostly related to study, technology, time management, social, communication and language skills. They can also include basic character traits such as honesty and talents related to subject areas like math or art. Identify your strengths at school and outside of school then write your strengths in the spaces on the wheel below.

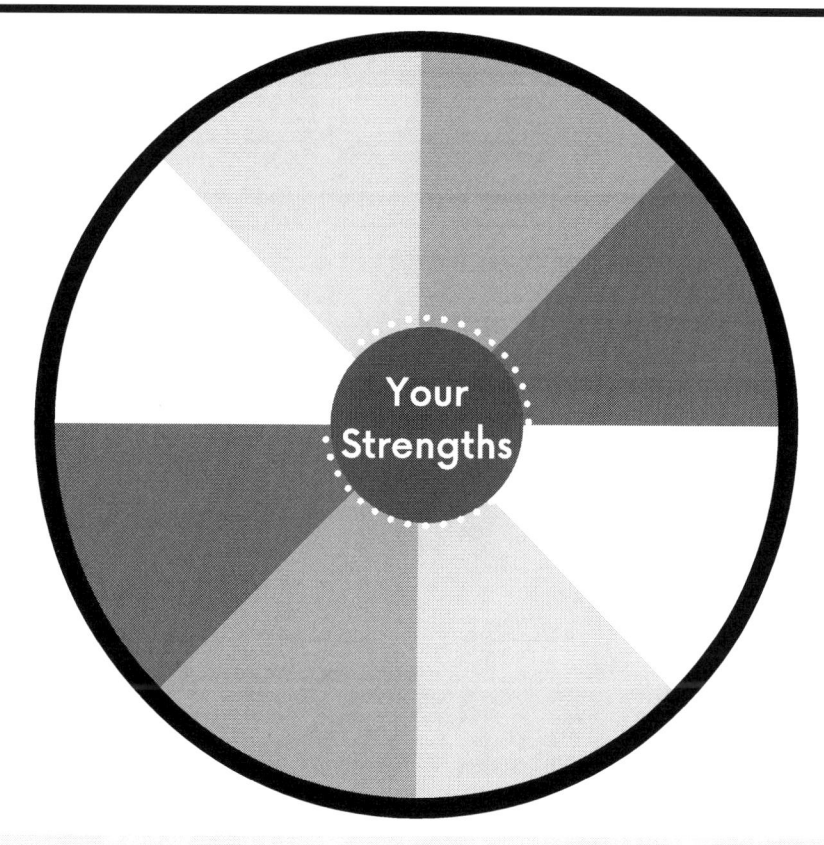

Your Strengths

Think about how you will bring these strengths with you to college. How can you use them? How can you continue improving on them? How can you use your strengths to contribute to your campus community?

EXCLUSIVE WORKBOOK ACTIVITY:
Basics in Money Management

Topic Information

Expenses and little purchases can add up quickly at college. Students often find themselves in trouble when they get into habits of buying food, pizza, snacks and delivery for themselves, their roommate and friends. In addition, costs can really add up when you make small purchases like a bag of chips from the vending machine, whereas buying an economy-sized bag at the grocery store would be cheaper. If you are living on campus you will likely already be paying for a meal plan... use it! **To highlight the differences, find the price of the items below and write the cost in the space to the right.**

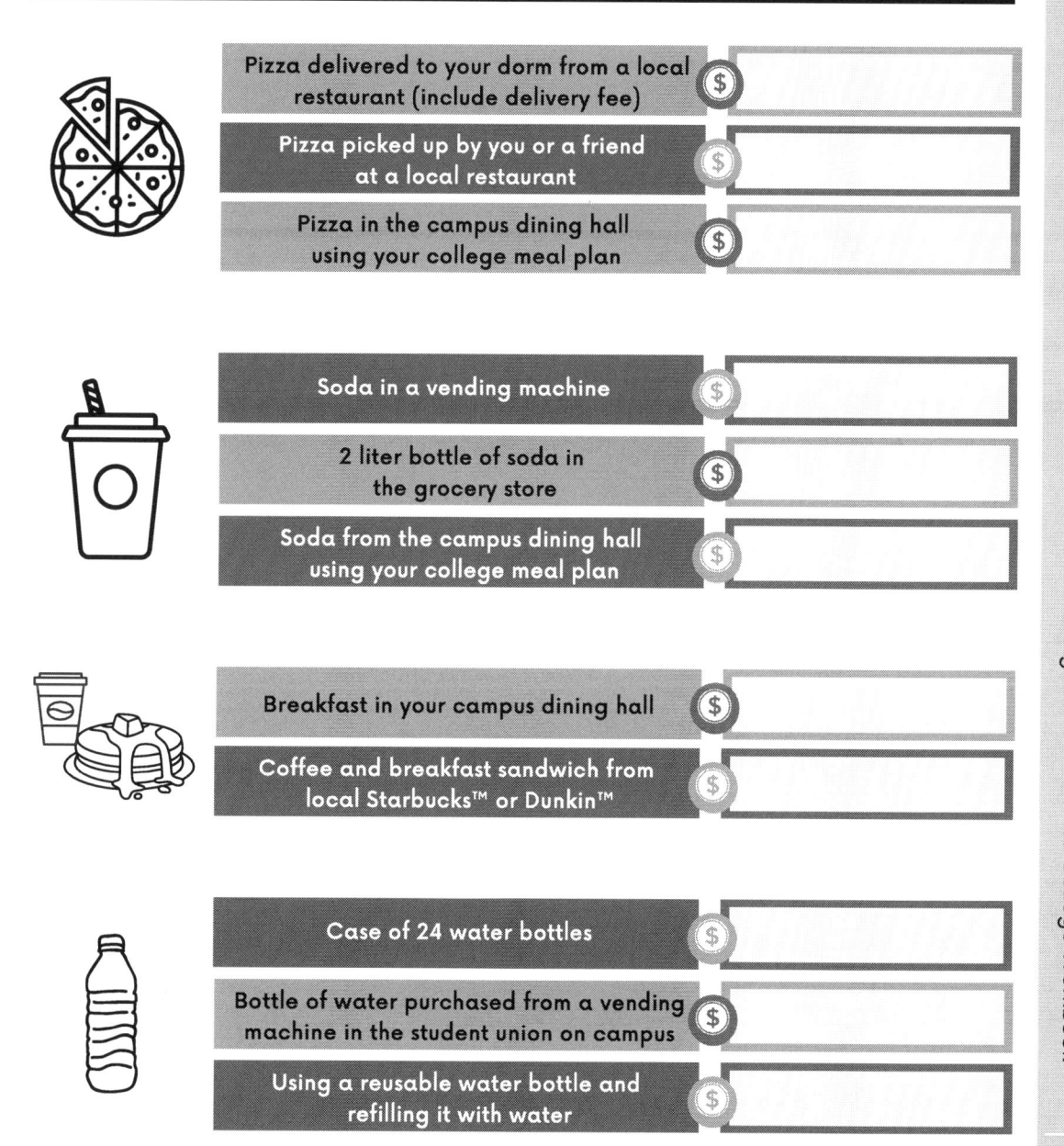

Item	$
Pizza delivered to your dorm from a local restaurant (include delivery fee)	
Pizza picked up by you or a friend at a local restaurant	
Pizza in the campus dining hall using your college meal plan	

Item	$
Soda in a vending machine	
2 liter bottle of soda in the grocery store	
Soda from the campus dining hall using your college meal plan	

Item	$
Breakfast in your campus dining hall	
Coffee and breakfast sandwich from local Starbucks™ or Dunkin™	

Item	$
Case of 24 water bottles	
Bottle of water purchased from a vending machine in the student union on campus	
Using a reusable water bottle and refilling it with water	

EXCLUSIVE WORKBOOK ACTIVITY:
Don't Forget To Meet The Deadlines

Topic Information

Deadlines are essential. If you don't apply for housing before the deadline, your options will be severely limited, and in some cases, nonexistent. When registering for classes each semester, you will need to register by the deadline or there might not be spots left in the classes you want to take. Think about the deadlines or important dates you have now in high school.

Use the space below to depict your system or strategies that help you remember important dates, deadlines & responsibilities

If remembering deadlines is a challenge for you, think of a few ways you can begin to work on that now to improve those skills:

_____
_____
_____

EXCLUSIVE WORKBOOK ACTIVITY:
What Is Your Communication Style?

Topic Information

Communication is critical. When it comes to key issues like sleeping, studying, and socializing, it's wise to communicate with your roommate about your preferences. Communication with professors and campus staff is also important. Use the scales below to rate yourself on your communication skills. Make sure you rate yourself <u>where you are, not where you want to be.</u>

Communication Statements	Disagree	Not Sure	Agree
I have difficulty making decisions	○	○	○
It's easy to voice my opinion even when others disagree with me	○	○	○
I feel anxious talking to teachers	○	○	○
I feel comfortable asking teachers questions	○	○	○
I feel comfortable telling others when I'm upset	○	○	○
I feel comfortable telling others when I'm sad	○	○	○
I feel nervous speaking up for myself when others disrespect me	○	○	○
I feel confident being in a leadership position	○	○	○
I prefer to be a follower than be a leader	○	○	○
I'm comfortable asking for directions if I don't know where I'm going	○	○	○

⚠️ <u>Pro Tip:</u> If you struggled answering these questions, talk to a friend, teacher, coach or parent and ask their feedback on your communication style and skills. They will be able to give you their thoughts, observations and even some pointers to improve!

EXCLUSIVE WORKBOOK ACTIVITY:
Stress is Normal. Let's Talk About it!

Topic Information

College can be challenging for everyone, and at some point in your college career you will probably experience stress, anger, or feel overwhelmed. It is completely normal to feel these emotions during college. Think about how you cope with feelings of stress, anxiety, being overwhelmed or angry now. Then think about going to college and identify situations where you might feel stressed and identify coping strategies you could use in those future situations.

Identify two situations in college that could potentially cause you stress

1. _____
2. _____

Your first year of college will be filled with bumps in the road which might cause some stress, so it is important to think about coping strategies now so you are more prepared for stressful situations.

What do you do to cope and work through stressful situaitons now?

_____
_____
_____

Which coping strategies would you use when confronting the potential stressful situations at college you listed above?

_____
_____
_____
_____
_____

EXCLUSIVE WORKBOOK ACTIVITY:
Discipline vs. Distractions

> *Discipline is Remembering What You Want*

What do you think this quote means?

_____
_____

Distractions will always be a part of life. If we choose to become distracted instead of acting with discipline our feelings in the moment become more important than the goals that we set for ourselves. Explain how the quote above can relate to distractions.

_____
_____
_____
_____

Are there distractions that typically keep you from your goals? Write them below:

How can you incorporate the quote above into your own life now or in the future at college?

EXCLUSIVE WORKBOOK ACTIVITY:
Problem Solving in College – Part One

Topic Information

Problem solving is an important life skill that will help you whether you are in college or in the workplace. Your science classes probably taught you the scientific method as one way to find solutions to problems, but you can use other personal qualities and traits to help you solve problems too. Have you ever used reasoning, flexibility, empathy or creativity to solve a problem? Read the scenarios below and think about how you would solve each problem.

What I Would Do

Scenario: You need to print out an assignment for class, but you have trouble connecting your computer to the library printer.

> I would ask for help from a librarian or IT staff member

Scenario: Your roommate leaves your dorm room unlocked when they leave for class, but you like to keep it locked.

Scenario: One of your class accommodations is access to class notes, but your professor has not given you a copy of their lecture notes yet.

Scenario: Your professor asks you to submit an assignment on Canvas or Blackboard (similar to Google Classroom). You finish the assignment but can't find where to submit it online.

EXCLUSIVE WORKBOOK ACTIVITY:
Problem Solving in College – Part Two

Topic Information

Problem solving is an important life skill that will help you whether you are in college or in the workplace. Your science classes probably taught you the scientific method as one way to find solutions to problems, but you can use other personal qualities and traits to help you solve problems too. Have you ever used reasoning, flexibility, empathy or creativity to solve a problem? Read the scenarios below and think about how you would solve each problem.

Scenario: Your roommate leaves garbage and clothes on your side of the dorm room.

What I Would Do

Scenario: Your roommate has an online class at the same time as your online class. You both sit at your desks and watch/listen to your online class, but it is loud in the room and you can't concentrate.

Scenario: Your roommate goes to bed before you do and asks you to be quiet, but you want to keep watching the movie that's half over on your computer.

EXCLUSIVE WORKBOOK ACTIVITY:
Express Yourself: Forward Thinking

Prompt: Imagine yourself 4 years from now...

Questions to get you started: What will you be doing? What will you have accomplished? What important people will be in your life? How will you feel?

Draw pictures, shapes or words in the space below

EXCLUSIVE WORKBOOK ACTIVITY:
College Website Scavenger Hunt

Topic Information

Colleges put a lot of time and effort into making their websites as user friendly and informative as possible. Get to know your college or university website - there is tons of helpful information on it! The college's website will likely be your first resource when you have a question or need quick information.

Activity: Complete this scavenger hunt for a college of your choice. Explore by clicking around the website or use the search bar on the website to find the answers below:

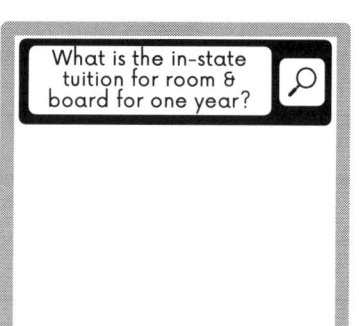

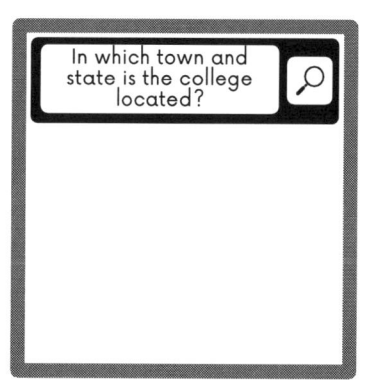

- What is the Application deadline?
- What is the in-state tuition for room & board for one year?
- What is the out-of-state tuition for room & board for one year?
- How many athletic teams does the campus have?
- In which town and state is the college located?
- What is the phone number for Campus Safety?
- Does the campus have a medical doctor on staff?
- Does the campus have a tutoring center? What is the name of the Director?

EXCLUSIVE WORKBOOK ACTIVITY:
Dealing With Noise In Your Residence Hall

Topic Information

If you decide to live on campus you will be living in a building with many other students who are just as excited as you to experience college life. Students come from all different backgrounds, home environments, and have different perceptions of reasonable noise levels. You should expect that because you are living with others around the same age that things have the potential to get pretty noisy. Most residence halls observe 'Quiet Hours' and have processes in place if students repeatedly violate that policy. It is likely there will be music, yelling, or laughing at all hours of the day and night to which you you may need to adapt and ensure you are courteous of others when it comes to your noise.

Here are some typical noises to expect in a college residence hall:

- Students walking loudly down the hallway
- Your roommate snoring
- Your roommate talking to their BF/GF/Partner
- Loud videos or FaceTime conversations
- Friends laughing loudly
- Loud music & wall-shaking bass

Activity: *Think about what you can do when your residence hall is noisy*

✏️ What are two things you could say?
_____
_____

✏️ What are two things you could do?
_____
_____

✏️ What rules related to noise are listed in your Residence Hall Policies?
_____
_____

Pro Tip: ⚠️ Consider buying earplugs to help block out noise while you sleep. There are also many apps for your phone that have white noise, music and relaxing sounds to help block out college residence hall noise.

Workbook Exclusive Handouts

EXCLUSIVE WORKBOOK HANDOUT:
Daily Planner

Date: _____
M T W T F S S

Quote of the day

Mood

Top 3 Priorities
- ☐ _____
- ☐ _____
- ☐ _____

Appointments
- ☐ _____
- ☐ _____
- ☐ _____

Things To Get Done
- ☐ _____
- ☐ _____
- ☐ _____
- ☐ _____
- ☐ _____
- ☐ _____
- ☐ _____
- ☐ _____

Things to Buy Today
- ☐ _____
- ☐ _____
- ☐ _____

Did I Exercise Today?
1. _____ Total Mins: _____
2. _____ Total Mins: _____
3. _____ Total Mins: _____

What Did I Eat Today?
Breakfast _____
Lunch _____
Dinner _____
Snacks _____

How Much Water Did I Drink?
💧 💧 💧 💧 💧
💧 💧 💧 💧

Notes:

Habits & Routines
1. _____ ☐
2. _____ ☐
3. _____ ☐
4. _____ ☐
5. _____ ☐
6. _____ ☐

EXCLUSIVE WORKBOOK HANDOUT:
Weekly Planner

My Week Month _____ Week _____

Monday
_____
_____
_____
_____
Grateful For: _____

Tuesday
_____
_____
_____
_____
Grateful For: _____

Weekly Goals
- _____
- _____
- _____
- _____
- _____
- _____
- _____
- _____
- _____

Wednesday
_____
_____
_____
_____
Grateful For: _____

Thursday
_____
_____
_____
_____
Grateful For: _____

Daily Tasks

	M	T	W	T	F	S	S

Friday
_____
_____
_____
_____
Grateful For: _____

This Weekend
_____
_____
_____
_____
Grateful For: _____

Notes:

EXCLUSIVE WORKBOOK HANDOUT:
Executive Functioning

6 Easy Strategies for Teachers & Parents to Improve a Student's Executive Functioning Skills

Provide time to organize at the end of a lesson or class

Keep supplies, papers, & books in the same place all the time

Give regular time checks

Encourage frequent de-cluttering days/times

Be explicit in your own executive functioning strategies

Intentionally point out when you are giving important info that requires students' attention

EXCLUSIVE WORKBOOK HANDOUT:
College Disability Support Services

> Having a disability doesn't define who you are or limit your potential. Support services at your college or university assist students and can help you succeed both personally and academically.

1. Registering for accommodations

To pursue accommodations or services at the college level, you must register as a student with a disability. This should take place soon after you have accepted admission to college. Contact the disability support services or Accessibility Office to find out the accommodation process and any documentation requirements.

2. Accommodations may be different from high school

Do not expect to have the same accommodations in college as you did in high school. In high school, you were provided with accommodations to ensure your participation in the general curriculum. In college, you must initiate the process to receive accommodations.

3. Common college accommodations

Some of the more common accommodations offered through colleges may include: priority registration, permission to record lectures, extended time on tests, testing in a limited-distraction environment, note taker for lectures, preferential seating, specialized fire alarms for those who are deaf or hard of hearing, and sign language interpreting services.

4. Disability documentation

Most colleges, if not all, will require you to provide documentation of your disability to receive accommodations. By researching these requirements, you will be able to gather the needed information in a timely manner.

5. Procedures to request accommodations

The college you attend will require you to follow procedures to request accommodations. It is up to you to know and monitor the process. Visit your college's Accessibility Office website, and review the specific information regarding the registration process.

6. Meet with disability services

Make an appointment to meet with a representative from the Disability/Accessibility Office well in advance of the start of the semester to review your documentation, discuss your individual needs and determine if you are eligible for services.

7. You are responsible for requesting accommodations

You are the person responsible for communicating your accommodation needs with each instructor. Meet with each of your instructors and share your accommodation letter with them. Start practicing now, while in high school. Request accommodations in class and actively participate in your IEP meetings.

EXCLUSIVE WORKBOOK HANDOUT:
Sample Accommodations Letter

Once you have been admitted to college, an important next step is to connect with the Accessibility/Disability office on your campus. Meeting with a member of the Accessibility Office staff and providing necessary documentation are the first steps to eligibility for appropriate academic and residential accommodations. The Accessibility Office will create an official letter outlining your approved accommodations that you can share with professors and housing staff. Below is a sample accommodations letter to give you an idea of what to expect.

Student Name: Mya Smith
Student ID: 0987654

Dear Professor,

The University of Fakeville provides reasonable and appropriate accommodations in accordance with federal and state law including the Americans with Disabilities Act and Section 504 of the Rehabilitation Act. The above-named student has provided documentation to Accessibility Services verifying eligibility of a disability.

The purpose of accommodations is to create equal educational access in accordance with state and federal regulations. In providing an accommodation this college is not required to modify essential requirements of a course or fundamentally alter the nature of a service program or activity.

It is the student's responsibility to meet with the faculty member in a timely manner to discuss the accommodations outlined below. The accommodations should not contradict the stated objectives and essential requirements of the course.

The student is eligible for the following accommodations:

Testing / Extended Time (50%)
   Student receives 1.5x (50%) additional time for timed assessments

Testing / Reduced Distraction Environment
   Student is able to take tests in the Disability Services office.

Classroom / Audio-record class lecture
   Due to a verified disability, this student is approved to audio record this class. A separate audiotaping agreement has been signed by the student and is on file with Accessibility Services.

If you have questions about this accommodation letter please contact the Accessibility Services office at (860) 123-4567 or email accessibilityoffice@fakecollege.com

EXCLUSIVE WORKBOOK HANDOUT:
Examples of College Accommodations

There are many different ways students can be supported with specific accommodations based on their ability to aid in success both in and out of the classroom. Below are some examples of accommodations students may be granted. You should work with the Accessibility Office to learn more about what options are available on your campus. Student support services are constantly evolving.

Testing Accommodations

- Extended time
- Use of computer for exams
- Clarified directions
- Distraction-reduced environment
- Alternate version/electronic textbooks
- Use of Speech-to-Text software
- Use of Text-to-Speech software
- Test question reader
- Scribes for Scantron bubble tests
- Wheelchair-accessible testing locations
- Permission to take medications or eat during exams
- Braille or large-print exam booklets

Classroom Accommodations

- Copies of presentation materials
- Designated note taker
- Preferential seating
- Enlarged print worksheets
- Recording of lectures
- Classroom location & furniture
- Smart devices to aid in note taking and typing
- Interpreting/Captioning

Housing & Dining Accommodations

- Specific building & room location
- Access to elevators
- Single room (medical reasons)
- Air Conditioning (medical reasons)
- Private bathroom (medical reasons)
- Special dietary needs
- Visual or physical fire alarms
- Furniture adjustments
- Service or support animals

Ask the Pros!
The staff at the Accessibility Office are experts in accommodations. Work with them to learn more about what options are available for you on your campus!

EXCLUSIVE WORKBOOK HANDOUT:
Make Your Goals S M A R T

> Setting goals can be a great way to challenge yourself to make healthy lifestyle changes. Set yourself up for success by making your goals **SMART**!

Specific
What is your goal?

Measurable
How will you keep track of progress?

Attainable
How will you reach your goal? Make a plan!

Relevant
How will this goal help you?

Timely
When will you achieve this goal?

S — My goal is: _____

M — I will track my progress by: _____

A — I will reach this goal by doing the following: _____

R — This goal helps me because: _____

T — I will complete this goal by (date): _____

EXCLUSIVE WORKBOOK HANDOUT:
Not-To-Do List

> As a student, you hear a lot about "To-do" lists and managing everything you need to remember and complete. Have you ever thought about making a "Not-To-Do" list? What are some things you are doing currently that get in your way of accomplishing your goals or feeling physically & mentally well?

Things that waste my time or distract me	Things that give me anxiety or stress me out
Things that drain my energy	Things I feel obligated to do
Things that don't actually need to be done	Things I can't control or aren't my responsibility

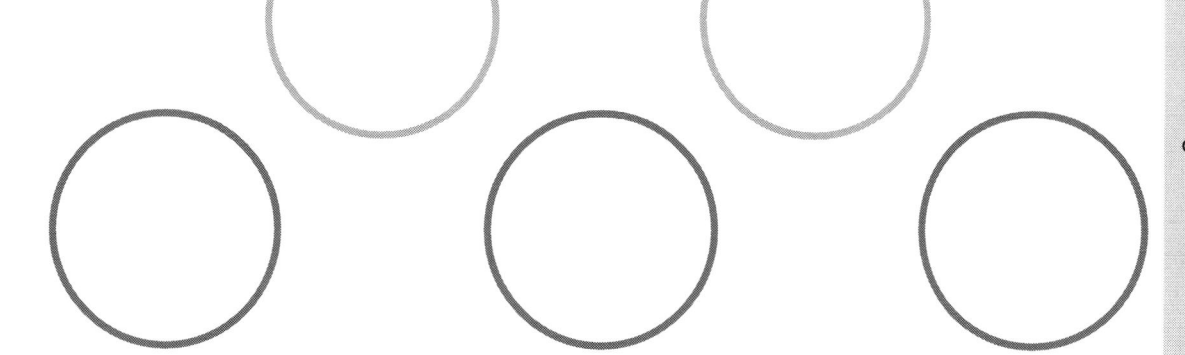

Top 5 Things I Need To Stop Doing

EXCLUSIVE WORKBOOK HANDOUT:
Semester Class Schedule

	Monday	Tuesday	Wednesday	Thursday	Friday
8:00am					
9:00am					
10:00am					
11:00am					
12:00pm					
1:00pm					
2:00pm					
3:00pm					
4:00pm					
5:00pm					
6:00pm					
7:00pm					
8:00pm					

EXCLUSIVE WORKBOOK HANDOUT:
College Application Tracker

Keeping track of all of the materials required when applying to each college can sometimes feel overwhelming, but it can be less stressful if you stay organized. Use the chart below to fill out what you will need for each college application, then check off each item as you complete it. Check off the "Application Complete" box once you have gathered all the required materials and submitted your application.

College/University	Deadline	App Fee	SAT/ACT Required	# Of Rec Letters	Transcripts	Common App or Writing Requirements	Application Complete
Example: Dream University	Jan 4	$75	Yes	2	Sent	Personal Essay	✓
1.							○
2.							○
3.							○
4.							○
5.							○
6.							○
7.							○
8.							○
9.							○

EXCLUSIVE WORKBOOK HANDOUT:
Important Campus Contacts

Residence Hall Staff
RA's Name:
RA's Room Number:
Hall Director's Name:
Hall Director's Email:
Department Phone Number:
After-Hours Phone Number:
Department Website:

Campus Safety
Office Location:
Department Email:
Department Phone Number:
After-Hours Phone Number:
Department Website:

Academic Advising
Office Location:
Your Advisor:
Contact Email:
Department Phone Number:
Department Website:

Tutoring & Academic Support
Office Location:
Main Contact:
Contact Email:
Department Phone Number:
Department Website:

Counseling Center
Office Location:
Main Contact:
Contact Email:
Department Phone Number:
Department Website:

Student Health Center
Office Location:
Main Contact:
Contact Email:
Department Phone Number:
Department Website:

Other:
Office Location:
Main Contact:
Contact Email:
Department Phone Number:
Department Website:

Other:
Office Location:
Main Contact:
Contact Email:
Department Phone Number:
Department Website:

About the Authors

Jennifer Sullivan, M.S.

Jennifer Sullivan, M.S. is an educator and author of the book, Sharing the Transition to College: Words of Advice for Diverse Learners and Their Families. She is CEO of Fast Forward College Coaching and is a private executive functioning coach supporting high school and college students with learning disabilities, autism, ADD, ADHD and anxiety. Jennifer has worked in higher education for 20 years and offers workshops for high school students and their families to help them navigate the shift from 504/IEP to learning and disability supports in college. She found her passion for supporting students in the transition to college after working in a transition program in CT for ten years in the roles of learning specialist, faculty and Director of New Student Experience and Parent Programming. She is a sought after speaker at local and national conferences and provides professional development training and workshops on executive functioning and advising postsecondary pathways for students with 504/IEP to schools, educators and parent groups across the country. Jennifer Sullivan has a Master's Degree in Multicultural and Urban Education and an Assistive Technology certification. Learn more about Jennifer Sullivan and Fast Forward College Coaching: www.fastforwardcollegecoaching.com

Jacquelynn Connell, M.S. Ed.

Jacquelynn is a Higher Education professional who draws on over a decade of experience serving students at colleges and universities. Her work has covered a number of functional areas in Student Affairs including new student orientation, student events & activities, residence life, student leadership & involvement, service learning, student employee training, transition programming, student retention, and instructing first-year seminar courses. With a passion for student transition and leadership development through the lens of diversity, equity and inclusion, Jacquelynn is fulfilled knowing that she is making an impact and guiding students to build decision-making skills, compassion, personal responsibility, and confidence to go forward and become engaged and competent members of their communities. The first in her family to attend college, Jacquelynn holds a Master's in Student Affairs Administration in Higher Education from the University of Wisconsin-La Crosse and a Bachelor's in Communication & Public Relations from the University of Wisconsin-Green Bay.

Acknowledgements

Jen Shares Her Gratitude:

Thank you to the educators, counselors and professionals who provided feedback and helped shape the creation of this workbook. Your feedback and suggestions "from the front lines" of education will help students in your schools and beyond prepare for college success. To Jackie - Your vision brought to life words on a page. Thank you for being an amazing partner, friend and colleague. Your creativity is limitless. I am in awe of your talent. To Cindy Samul - Thank you for your time and talent on this project. To Mom, Dad and Becky - Thank you for your unwavering support and encouragement. I'm incredibly lucky and grateful to have you in my life. To Lana and Emily - I'm excited for your futures and hope these pages will help you both in your college journeys. To Ron - You are my everything. You inspire me to do and be more of who I am. Thank you for the space and support to pursue my passion.

Jackie Shares Her Gratitude:

Creating this workbook has been more rewarding than I could have ever imagined. None of this would have been possible without the vision and leadership of Jen. Thank you, Jen, for inviting me to collaborate on this incredible workbook and Fast Forward initiatives- your passion for diverse learners is inspiring. Throughout my career in Higher Education I have had the honor to work with incredible supervisors who saw potential in me, co-workers with whom I could laugh through the hard stuff, and students who have trusted me and taught me more than any classroom. I am so appreciative for the experiences and countless lessons learned along the way. Helping others and working hard was central to my upbringing and I want to share my appreciation with you, Dad & Mom, for the encouragement to continue my education, put family first always, and for your support to take big risks. To my sister, Stacy, and brother, Cody, the greatest gift our parents ever gave us was each other, and I am so thankful that our closeness remains as life gets more complex. Finally, and above all, I cannot begin to express my unfailing gratitude and love to my husband, Drew. You see me and have helped me see myself. You have supported me and my Student Affairs career (even when we lived on campus) and help me to keep things in perspective when doubt and anxiety feel insurmountable. I am eternally grateful.

Check Out The Book That Started It All!

An invaluable, thoughtfully written how-to guide filled with practical tips and words of advice for college-bound students and their families. This comprehensive guide offers guidance on how to smoothly navigate the complexities of the college transition. Providing reassurance, this book will help families be proactive, know what to expect and begin the college journey with confidence.

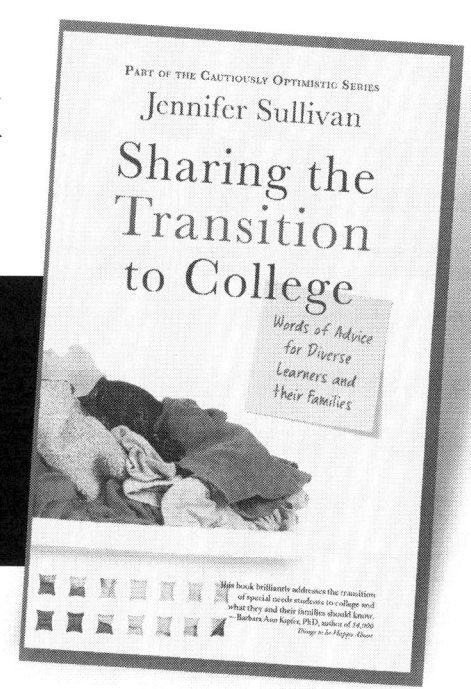

★★★★★ Reviews:

"Sharing the Transition to College" is a must-have resource for families & professionals. I highly recommend this comprehensive, easy to follow guide to students, families and educators. The practical tips and interactive activities keep the reader engaged and interested. The uses for this guide are endless! While some parents may choose to read it alongside their children, educators can also use it in an academic setting. I can't wait to share this new tool with my colleagues!"
  —Sara Alberti, Supervisor of Student Service and Special Education, Middletown Public Schools, CT

"College anxiety is real for students and their parents and exponentially more so for students with disabilities. This guide book is an excellent tool for young people and families to successfully maneuver the higher education journey. Ms. Sullivan provides valuable insight, information and support on how to let go and grow through this process!"
  —New Jersey parent of a diverse thinking college student

"This is a terrific book...exactly what every student - and parent - needs to make a successful transition to college. I highly recommend it and plan to use it as I counsel families and students who are moving beyond high school."
  —Susan Yellin, Director of Advocacy and Transition Services, The Yellin Center for Mind, Brain and Education and co-author of Life After High School: A Guide for Students with Disabilities and Their Families

"As an individual who works with students transitioning to college, I can say Jennifer Sullivan hit it out of the park with this terrific resource for students and families. I often find books on college to be overwhelming and Jennifer Sullivan has managed to create an easy read which packs information into every page."
  —Christopher Scott, Disability Service Professional, Center for Students with Disabilities, University of Connecticut

"I highly recommend this book, especially for parents - this is one of the few books I've seen that focuses on how parents can prepare both themselves and their student for a successful next step."
  —Massachusetts parent of a diverse learning college student

Fast Forward College Coaching /FastForwardCollegeCoaching
@jshighered contact@fastforwardcollegecoaching.com

FastForwardCollegeCoaching.com

Made in the USA
Middletown, DE
20 October 2023